Bharati Mukherjee

Twayne's United States Authors Series

Frank Day, Editor

Clemson University

TUSAS 653

BHARATI MUKHERJEE
Photograph © Jerry Bauer

Bharati Mukherjee

Fakrul Alam

University of Dhaka

Twayne Publishers
An Imprint of Simon & Schuster Macmillan
New York

Prentice Hall International
London • Mexico City • New Delhi • Singapore • Sydney • Toronto

Twayne's United States Authors Series No. 653

Bharati Mukherjee
Fakrul Alam

Twayne Publishers
An Imprint of Simon & Schuster Macmillan
866 Third Avenue
New York, New York 10022

Library of Congress Cataloging-in-Publication Data

Alam, Fakrul.
Bharati Mukherjee / Fakrul Alam.
    p.   cm. — (Twayne's United States authors series ; no. 653)
    Includes bibliographical references and index.
    ISBN 0-8057-3997-1
    1. Mukherjee, Bharati—Criticism and interpretation. 2. Women and literature—United States—History—20th century. 3. Women and literature—Canada—History—20th century. 4. Women and literature—India—History—20th century. 5. East Indian Americans in literature. 6. India—In literature. I. Title. II. series.
PR9499.3.M77Z516   1995
813'.54—dc20   95-10832
                                                                                                            CIP

10 9 8 7 6 5 4 3 2 1

Printed in the United States of America

To Frank Day

Contents

Preface

Bharati Mukherjee's four novels—*Holder of the World* (1993), *Jasmine* (1989), *Wife* (1975), and *The Tiger's Daughter* (1972)—two collections of short fiction—*The Middleman* (1988) and *Darkness* (1983)—and the prose essays and the two works of nonfiction she has produced in collaboration with her husband, Clark Blaise—*Days and Nights in Calcutta* (1977) and *The Sorrow and the Terror* (1987)—can be seen either as books by a leading writer of the Indian diaspora or as works by a prominent Asian-American writer. Mukherjee, however, has staked a claim for herself as an "Ellis Island writer," an American storyteller writing about the lives of new migrants to the United States.

As one of a new generation of Indian writers who have chosen to settle in the West and write in the English language, Mukherjee is in the company of writers such as Salman Rushdie, Rhonton Mistry, and Vikram Seth. As an Asian-American writer representing the experience of recent Asian immigrants or the evolution of migrant selves in North America, Mukherjee joins the likes of Maxine Hong Kingston and Diana Chang. But when Mukherjee characterizes herself as an "Ellis Island writer," she is self-consciously putting herself in the tradition best exemplified by Bernard Malamud, the writer to whom her first collection of fiction, *Darkness,* is dedicated.

I discuss Mukherjee's literary affiliations in the concluding chapter of this book; in the body of this study I analyze her fiction and nonfiction. As I see it, Mukherjee's work can be divided into four phases. The books of the first phase—*The Tiger's Daughter* and *Days and Nights in Calcutta*—contain fictional and nonfictional treatments of trips to India, the country where she was born and did most of her growing up. These books look at "home" from an exile's perspective. I examine these books in Chapter 2, where I also explore the nature of Mukherjee's current links to India.

Mukherjee gave up her Indian citizenship after moving to Canada with her Canadian husband and taking up a position at McGill University in 1966. Among her books that deal directly or indirectly with her experience of expatriation in Canada are *Wife, Darkness,* and *The Sorrow and the Terror,* although her sharpest response to her feelings about Canada is perhaps her essay "An Invisible Woman." I examine these works in Chapter 3, where I also explore Mukherjee's exasperation with Canada's policy of multiculturalism, which she felt relegated its "colored" migrants to the condition of perpetual expatriates.

Mukherjee now considers herself as an immigrant American writer, and a reading of her recent nonfiction shows that she considers the fiction she has produced in the United States her most significant to date. Certainly, the two books she has produced in this phase of her career—*The Middleman* and *Jasmine*—have earned her the most attention she has received so far. Chapter 4 addresses these works and explains why Mukherjee has been so enthusiastic about her move to the United States and why she has felt a heightening in her creative powers on account of this move.

In 1993 Mukherjee entered a new phase of her career with the publication of her fourth novel, *The Holder of the World,* which is concerned not so much with immigrants as with the spatiotemporal connections between cultures. I argue that by writing this novel Mukherjee attempts to place herself in the American tradition of prose narrative while affirming her origins in Indian artistic traditions.

Chapter 1 provides the facts needed to understand Bharati Mukherjee and her work. Mukherjee may see herself as an American writer, but the circumstances of her birth, upbringing, and education in India as much as her marriage to a North American and her education and career on the American continent are the indispensable contexts to an understanding of her fiction. Chapters 1 and 5, where I place her in larger contexts and evaluate her contribution to contemporary literature, frame the four central chapters of this study.

Acknowledgments

It is impossible to write about a contemporary American writer while working in Bangladesh without having to depend on correspondents, ex-students, and friends and relatives who live overseas and are able to send books, reviews, and essays, but it is a pleasure to record their help. I owe special thanks to Tahseen Ishtiaque Alam, Khawja Moinul Hassan, Emmanuel S. Nelson, Ralph J. Crane, Ian Ross, and Rezina Wahed for volunteering or responding so graciously and promptly to my requests for material indispensable to the writing of this book. I am grateful, too, to my wife, Nazma Alam, and my sister and brother-in-law, Dr. Momtaz Islam and Dr. Azharul Islam, for their emotional support. Farhad Bin Idris and Hasnain Atique read portions of the manuscript and saved me from many errors of expression. To Barbara Sutton I must acknowledge my indebtedness for her editorial skills. Hasnain Atique also helped immensely with his word-processing skills and resources. To Mark Zadrozny of Twayne Publishers, I am thankful for his patience and understanding. My chief debt, however, is to Frank Day, for he has not only sent me material, but has also been consistently helpful, supportive, and patient, and it is fitting that I should acknowledge it by dedicating this book to him.

Chronology

1940   Bharati Mukherjee born in Calcutta, India, on 27 July, the second of three daughters of Sudhir Lal Mukherjee, a chemist, and Bina Mukherjee.

1947   India becomes independent; the Mukherjee family moves to England, where Sudhir Lal Mukherjee is engaged in research.

1951   The Mukherjees return to Calcutta. The girls attend Loreto Convent School, an exclusive private school run by Irish nuns.

1959   Bharati Mukherjee receives a B.A. (with honors) in English from the University of Calcutta. Leaves Calcutta for Baroda, a city in western India, where her father has found employment.

1961   Mukherjee receives an M.A. in English and ancient Indian culture from the University of Baroda.

1962   Travels to the United States on a PEO International Peace Scholarship to attend the University of Iowa's Writer's Workshop.

1963   Receives M.F.A. from the University of Iowa.

1964   Marries Clark Blaise, a Canadian-American fellow student at the Writer's Workshop.

1964–1965   Instructor in English at Marquette University, Milwaukee, and the University of Wisconsin-Madison.

1966   Moves to Montreal to teach at McGill University, where she will work her way up from being a lecturer to a full professor by 1978, and where she will teach till 1980.

1969   Receives Ph.D. in English and comparative literature from the University of Iowa.

1972   *The Tiger's Daughter.*

1973   Spends a year in India on a sabbatical with her husband. Begins work on *Wife.* Receives Canada Arts Council grant.

1975   *Wife* published and is a finalist for the Governor General's Award of Canada.

1977   *Days and Nights in Calcutta,* written in collaboration with Clark Blaise, published. Receives Canada Arts Council grant.

1978–1979   Receives Guggenheim Foundation Award.

1980   Moves to New York, becomes a permanent U.S. resident, embarks on a free-lance teaching career. Teaches at Skidmore College, Mountain State College, Queen's College of the City University of New York, and Columbia University. Receives first prize from Periodical Distributor's Association for short story "Isolated Incidents."

1981   Receives National Magazine Awards second prize for the essay "An Invisible Woman."

1984–1987   Is associate professor at Mountain State College in New Jersey.

1984   Is writer-in-residence at Emory University, where, in a burst of creativity, she writes most of the stories collected in *Darkness.*

1985   *Darkness.*

1986   Receives National Endowment for the Arts grant.

1987   Is professor at City University of New York. Publishes *The Sorrow and the Terror,* another collaborative work with Clark Blaise, on an Air India plane crash. "The Tenant" chosen for inclusion in *Best American Short Stories of 1987.*

1988   *The Middleman and Other Stories.* Receives 1988 National Book Critics Circle Award for fiction.

1989   *Jasmine.* Moves to California to become distinguished professor at Berkeley.

1993   *The Holder of the World* published.

Chapter One

Introduction

Bharati Mukherjee was born on 27 July 1940 in Calcutta, India. Her father, Sudhir Lal Mukherjee, was a chemist of some distinction who had studied and done advanced research in Germany and the United Kingdom. Her mother, Bina Mukherjee, was not particularly educated, as was the case with most Bengali women of her generation, but she and her husband made sure that their three daughters received the best education possible. A consequence was that Mukherjee and her two sisters all did postgraduate work and ended up as academics.

The Mukherjees were Bengali Brahmins—that is, members of the highest caste among Bengali Hindus. Sudhir Mukherjee's ancestral home was in Faridpur and his wife's in Dhaka, two districts of Bengal that became part of East Pakistan (now Bangladesh) when the province was partitioned at the time of India's independence in 1947. Their families had moved to Calcutta, as did many other educated, high-caste Hindus in the first of the many diasporas associated with Bharati Mukherjee's life. In Calcutta she grew up in an extended family, surrounded by uncles and aunts and cousins, one of about 40 residents of the joint family home in Calcutta's middle-class Rash Behari Avenue.

The dominant influence on Mukherjee's early years was her father. Sudhir Mukherjee, who died in 1985, was energetic and gregarious, a larger-than-life character who became the model for the "Tiger" of her first novel, *The Tiger's Daughter*. As Mukherjee remembers him in an interview given to *Canadian Fiction Magazine,* he was "an extraordinary man . . . very much the benevolent patriarch" who "wanted the best for his daughters. And to him, the 'best' meant intellectually fulfilling lives."[1]

On his return from England, where he had gotten a Ph.D. from the University of London, Sudhir Mukherjee had set a pharmaceuticals business in Calcutta, taking as his partner a Jewish immigrant from the Middle East. Their business flourished until the partners quarrelled, soon after India achieved independence in 1947. Sudhir Mukherjee then left for London to do research on his own, taking with him his wife and daughters. The partner, however, pursued him to England, apologized, and asked him to continue his research project in the West on the company's behalf for the time being. Bharati Mukherjee therefore spent a portion of her childhood in London and in Basel, Switzerland, where her father also did some scientific work.

In 1951 Sudhir Mukherjee returned to Calcutta to take up an active role in the business, now booming because of the success of drugs he had invented for it. He decided, however, not to take his family back to the joint family house—a move Mukherjee has described in one of the many autobiographical sections of *Days and Nights in Calcutta,* the book about her year-long sojourn in Calcutta, which she wrote with her husband Clark Blaise, as a release from a "terrifying communal bonding."[2] Instead, he settled his family in a mansion in the factory compound, complete with a swimming pool, a lake, armed guards, and a retinue of servants. These were the golden years of Bharati Mukherjee's childhood, made possible by her father's success as a businessman as well as a scientist. But the years spent in the West and the life the family lived within the walled compound meant that the daughters were becoming increasingly alienated from the middle-class Calcutta of their early childhood. As Mukherjee sees it, the family had now "refused to merge with the city," having decided to embark on the route that would eventually make them all leave it and settle in far-off places (*Days,* 185).

Sudhir Mukherjee himself left Calcutta when another quarrel with his partner and the litigation that followed made him think of starting his career anew in another part of India. He eventually resettled himself and his family in the western Indian city of Baroda, where he became the research director of the pharmaceuticals division of a large chemical company. In 1967 he had to move again, this time to Chembur, a place just outside Bombay, where he was made the head of the company's plastic division. By this time his daughters had all left home, having completed their education and married. But although his daughters had decided to marry out of love and not let their fates be decided by marriages arranged by their father as is traditional in India, Sudhir Mukherjee had exerted a decisive influence on their lives. Thus he seemed to have shaped Bharati Mukherjee's decision to be a writer, not only by imbuing her with his belief "in the power of the word" (1987 interview, 39) but also by taking the initiative in sending her off to the Writer's Workshop at the University of Iowa. *Days and Nights in Calcutta* contains affectionate glimpses of Sudhir Mukherjee, etched by both Bharati Mukherjee and her husband, and shows him at home in Chembur, no longer the "Tiger" but a caring father and a religious man.

As for Bharati Mukherjee's mother, she was a quiet but solid presence in the lives of the daughters. In the interview published in *Canadian Fiction Magazine,* Mukherjee characterizes Bina Mukherjee as "one of those exceptional Third World women who 'burned' all her life for an education, which was denied to well-brought-up women of her generation," a mother who "made sure" that her daughters "never suffered the same wants" (1987 interview, 31). In *Days and Nights in Calcutta* Mukherjee records a more specific debt when she recalls how her mother was "a powerful storyteller" who "did not care about precise statistics, only about passion" (173). Furthermore, Bharati Mukherjee tells us that although she admired her father, she was physically and temperamentally closer to her mother. Thus she looked like Bina Mukherjee and is, like her, "a collector of resentments and insults, and stubbornly unforgiving" (180). Perhaps this aspect of her character comes out clearly in the bitterness that still rankles her when she thinks about her years in Canada.

Bina Mukherjee played a major role in her daughters' upbringing on many occasions. For instance, it was her determination to see her daughters independent and safe from the humiliations often suffered by middle-class women in traditional Hindu marriages that led her to "make sure they're well educated so no one can make them suffer" (*Days,* 228). It was in keeping with this resolution that Bina Mukherjee decided to send her daughters to an Anglicized Bengali school—as opposed to schools where the only medium of instruction was the vernacular language, Bengali—and to supervise their reading and writing, unwittingly engendering in Bharati Mukherjee in the process a loss of faith in Calcutta and a dream of making "a foreign continent" her "battleground for proving self-worth" (*Days,* 229).

Bharati Mukherjee grew up in an "extraordinarily close-knit family" (*Days,* 182). This, and the lives they led within the walled compound of the factory, made the Mukherjee girls feel "inviolable and inaccessible" (*Days,* 183). Although her parents were traditional and orthodox in most of their beliefs—to this day Bharati Mukherjee retains a belief in the Hinduism taught to her by them—in other ways they had fostered in their daughters qualities that would lead Bharati to break away from family and country. Their desire to make their daughters get an Anglicized education, to seek careers outside their homes, and to pursue independent, self-fulfilling lives meant that Bharati Mukherjee would eventually leave them and India for a life abroad and for the profession of a writer-academic.

Education

When she was three years old, Bharati Mukherjee was sent to a bilingual school run by Protestant missionaries. The medium of instruction here was Bengali, but more emphasis was put on English than in other Bengali-medium institutions of the city. When the family shifted to England in 1947, Mukherjee and her sisters were admitted to a small private school in London, where they first became fluent in English and distinguished themselves by "carrying off [all] the prizes" (*Days*, 27). The Western education continued when they were admitted to a German school in Basel. The return to Calcutta in 1951, however, did not mean a return to a bilingual education; not only had the family now settled in a mansion walled off from the city, but also the girls were placed in the exclusive Loreto Convent School, which Mukherjee has described as a school run by Irish nuns who regarded the "walled-off school compound in Calcutta as a corner (forever green and tropical) of England."[3] The fact that the sisters would be chauffeured to the school miles away from home in a car with a bodyguard and at times an escort vehicle in front of it to protect them from the violence that was then becoming endemic in Calcutta also meant that Mukherjee was now living at a further remove from everyday Calcutta life as well as Bengali culture, which the nuns were teaching her to "devalue." This, of course, was a situation bound to create "complications."[4] Unlearning Bengali traditions and learning to be English, performing in Gilbert and Sullivan operettas, and practicing English elocution lessons made Bharati fast become part of "a class that did not live in its native language" ("Woman," 24). To put it somewhat differently, the process through which Mukherjee would eventually be uprooted from her country, begun when the family had moved to London, accelerated in her high school years.

After graduating from the Loreto Convent School, Bharati earned a B.A. (with honors) in English from the University of Calcutta in 1959. She then went with her father to Baroda. At the University of Baroda she earned an M.A. in English and ancient Indian culture. She now realizes that the education she received in Baroda, which involved studying her country's heritage, was invaluable, for it helped offset somewhat the very Anglicized schooling she had been getting till then and reinforced the religious principles that had been inculcated in her by her parents, both devout Hindus. These principles are still of some importance to Mukherjee, and she has tried to make creative use of such Hindu beliefs as the idea of reincarnation in works such as *Jasmine*.

Mukherjee had wanted to be a writer from an early age and had even written 60 or 80 pages of a novel about English children when she was in London and not yet in her teens. At the Loreto Convent School she had written short stories for the school magazine, *Palm Leaves,* in which she fictionalized episodes from European history. By the time she was in college she had decided to become a writer and not a scientist like her father. It was a decision that Sudhir Mukherjee endorsed, and it was he who in 1960 sought out a visiting American academic to find out where he could send his daughter for formal training in fiction. At the American professor's suggestion, he sent a letter to the poet Paul Engle, then in the Creative Writing Program in Iowa. The letter, and a recommendation from another visiting American scholar, was enough to get Bharati Mukherjee admission and a scholarship to do graduate work in the United States. And so in September 1961 she found herself in the University of Iowa's Writer's Workshop, propelled by her desire to be a writer and her father's ambition to leave her country for a North American education. This was, of course, the second time in her life that she had come to live in the West, but on this occasion she was there all by herself and would not be going back to resettle in India again. Mukherjee earned an M.F.A. from the University of Iowa in 1963. For her thesis she had submitted a collection of short fiction. She had evidently impressed the English Department faculty, for they admitted her to their doctoral program (she earned a Ph.D. in English and comparative literature in 1969).

Career

Bharati Mukherjee has been able to combine successfully her vocation for writing with her training in English and comparative literature. Her academic career began in 1964 when she moved to Wisconsin to be an instructor in English, at first at Marquette University and then at the University of Wisconsin at Madison. In 1966 she and her husband joined the faculty of Montreal's McGill University. Beginning as a lecturer in this institution, Mukherjee moved up the academic ladder with impressive speed to become a full professor in 1978. While at McGill she published *The Tiger's Daughter* (1972), *Wife* (1975), and the collaborative *Days and Nights in Calcutta,* as well as a number of purely academic essays. She further distinguished herself during this period by serving for some time as the chair of McGill's writing program and as director of graduate studies in English. She also received a number of grants for her

work from McGill University (1968, 1970), the Canada Arts Council
(1973–74), and the Guggenheim Foundation (1978–79).

Despite such a successful career, Mukherjee was increasingly unhappy
with her life in Montreal. For reasons I discuss later in this chapter, she
and her husband decided to quit their jobs in McGill, preferring to free-
lance in the United States rather than to hold on to their tenured posi-
tions in Canada. For most of the 1980s, therefore, Mukherjee taught at a
number of institutions in and around New York City. She has taught at
Skidmore College (Saratoga Springs), Mountain State College, Queen's
College of the City University of New York, and Columbia University. In
1984 she was also writer-in-residence at Emory University. During this
period she published *Darkness* (1985), *The Middleman and Other Stories*
(1988), and another collaborative work with her husband on the 1985
bombing of an Air India jetliner, *The Sorrow and the Terror* (1987).
Mukherjee's big break as a writer came when she won the National Book
Critic Circle Award for fiction for *The Middleman and Other Stories*. The
volume, and her next novel, *Jasmine* (1989), were widely reviewed and
praised, and led to her being offered a Distinguished Professorship at
Berkeley. It was while teaching at Berkeley that Mukherjee wrote *The
Holder of the World* (1993). Mukherjee continues to teach in California,
although she spends a part of every year in New York and in Iowa, where
her husband has been teaching in the Writer's Workshop program.

Mukherjee has thus achieved remarkable success, both as a creative
writer and as a full-time academic. How has her teaching affected her
writing? In the interview published in *Canadian Fiction Magazine* she
points out that the demands of university teaching have, inevitably, con-
strained her somewhat: "If I could afford to live just on my writing, I
expect I'd be rather prolific." She goes on to emphasize, however, that
she likes to run fiction workshops since they give her "a chance to hone
my theories about writing" (1987 interview, 33). And while she has
taught traditional literature courses and has had to spend time on
administrative work, her published interviews and essays make clear that
she is the kind of writer who thrives in an academic environment.

Marriage

Mukherjee's marriage to the novelist-writer Clark Blaise has had a
major impact on her career as an academic and as an author. Although
they have raised two sons, they have had what Mukherjee has described
as "an intensely literary marriage."[5] Not surprisingly, husband and wife

have shaped each other's careers in quite tangible ways. For instance, Mukherjee moved to Canada in 1966 to teach at McGill at his insistence—he had felt at that time that he needed to go back to Canada to rediscover his roots, although she was reluctant to move north. On the other hand, Blaise left Montreal in 1980 because she wanted them to start anew in the United States.

Blaise was born in North Dakota in 1940 and grew up in Gainesville, Florida. He met Mukherjee soon after he joined Iowa's Writer's Workshop in February 1962 and married her one lunch hour in September 1963. Since then, they have lived together for most of the time, although the need to move where jobs were available meant that occasionally they have also had to live apart.

A proficient novelist and a frequently anthologized writer of fiction, Blaise has published two collections of short stories—*A North American Education* (1973) and *Tribal Justice* (1979)—two novels—*Lunar Attractions* (1979) and *Lusts* (1983)—and *Resident Aliens* (1986), a collection of short fiction and autobiographical essays. As the title of this last book indicates, Blaise has been interested like Mukherjee in the phenomenon of migration, the status of new immigrants, and the feeling of alienation often experienced by expatriates.

In her interviews Mukherjee has pointed out how Blaise's ideas about fiction and experience in teaching and writing fiction have been of help to her in her fiction. She has described him as "a very good audience for her work," someone who has been reading it and commenting on it ever since she graduated from the Writer's Workshop with him (1988 interview, 653). At times his advice has been crucial for her work. For example, when writing her first novel she could not make up her mind about inserting an episode where her heroine is seduced by a less-than-agreeable character because of her fears that people would conclude that something similar had happened to her. In the end, though, she retained the episode because Blaise insisted that "the novel demands it, and you have to go through with it" (1990 interview, 27).

Mukherjee has described the process of collaboration with Blaise on literary projects as "always exciting" (1987 interview, 36). Together the couple have produced two full-length books—*Days and Nights in Calcutta* and *The Sorrow and the Terror*—a longish essay on the controversial novelist Salman Rushdie's life after the publication of *The Satanic Verses,* and a screenplay based on *Days and Nights in Calcutta.* The nature of the collaboration, of course, has differed from project to project. Thus, the book on their sabbatical trip to India is a compilation of "separate accounts about overlapping experience," while the book on the Air India jetliner crash was a "more concerted" effort where every "single segment" had been worked on by both writers (1987 interview, 37).

Mukherjee has credited Blaise with helping her arrive at her aesthetic. In her *Iowa Review* interview she has said that she hit upon the key element of her poetics—"finding the right voice" as the controlling aspect of a work—by "talking to, or listening to" Blaise (1990 interview, 30). In the same interview she talks about how much she has learned about fiction and "the inventions of autobiography" from reading the essays in *Resident Aliens* (31).

Not that such an exceptional marriage between two writer-academics coming from such different backgrounds has not had its difficult moments. *Days and Nights in Calcutta* records with some intensity one such moment when husband and wife quarrel—a moment when she accuses him "of forcing expatriation" on her (*Days*, 221). She and her husband were in Calcutta at a critical moment of their married life, when she felt he was forcing her to live in Canada, to learn a new language, to adapt to new people, and to write for a new audience. When he tried to reply to her accusation, he pointed out how it would have been impossible for him to work in Calcutta, implying thereby that it was at least possible for her to do so in Canada. At this part of her narrative, Mukherjee records with compelling candor the limitations of having a North American as a husband when in India. No matter how decent a man he had turned out to be, he could not be expected to understand some of the complicated emotions she was experiencing about herself and her position as an expatriate on this visit to her homeland.

Reading Mukherjee's published comments about her marital life leaves one with no doubt that despite such moments, she and Blaise have had a very happy and fruitful relationship over the years. But there can be little doubt, too, that Mukherjee's feelings about the stresses and strains of such a cross-cultural relationship as well as its creative possibilities have been grist for her fictional mill.

Bharati Mukherjee and the Immigrant Experience

Even the most cursory survey of Mukherjee's upbringing, career, and marriage brings out the crucial fact about her background as a writer: her personal history consists of a series of displacements and expatriations. Part of the diaspora that has been a feature of the Indian subcontinent's history this century, she has traveled widely, moving from place to place, nation to nation, and even continent to continent, for one reason or the other. Quite understandably, then, as a writer she has been most interested in the phenomenon of migration, especially the migration of South Asians to the new world. Making the most of her experience as an immigrant, first in Canada and then in the United States, drawing on her knowledge of migrant lives and cross-cultural relationships, she has produced fiction not only about uprooted individuals, the anguish of expatriation, and the inevitable frustrations felt by immigrants trying to cope with loneliness and an often hostile culture, but also about the excitement of immigration, the sense of rebirth, and the expectations of a better life that are part of the immigrant experience.

Mukherjee's attitude toward exile, expatriation, and immigration has changed over the years. Although she now has a full and joyous sense of herself as "an immigrant, living in a continent of immigrants" (1987 interview, 32), she had at first felt like an exile, or at best an expatriate. As an exile, Mukherjee felt drawn to the country she had left behind and compelled from time to time to evaluate the nature of her ties to her "home." As an expatriate in Canada, she considered herself superior to immigrants, people who appeared to her as "lost souls, put upon and pathetic," while expatriates "knew all too well who and what they were, and what foul fate had befallen them."[6] Content to be an expatriate, she would, like V. S. Naipaul, one of her literary heroes of that period, look down on immigrants as "adrift souls in the new world, wondering if they could ever belong" (*Darkness,* 2).

Mukherjee's perspective on exile and on expatriates and immigrants began to change in the 1970s and for two reasons. One of the them was the year-long trip she took to Calcutta in 1973. As it ended, she realized that henceforth she would have to view herself "more as an immigrant than an exile" (*Days,* 284). Though she would return to India for more visits in the future, she had discovered in this sabbatical trip to India that "for all the troubles" she was undergoing in Canada, "it was still the new world that she wanted to live in." After much soul-searching about her links to India, she felt that the time had come for her to say, "the old world was dead for me" (1990 interview, 15).

"The trouble" that she was going through in Canada, however, was about to transform her attitude toward that country and toward expatriation and immigration. What Mukherjee is referring to here is her experience of racism in Canada. In the 1970s growing unemployment and increased emigration from Asia to that country led to a series of attacks on blacks, Indians, and Chinese immigrants in cities such as Vancouver,

Montreal, and Toronto. In "An Invisible Woman," an eloquent attack on Canada's policy of multiculturalism and an account of the way her experience of racism in Canada had unsettled her, Mukherjee describes the humiliations felt by herself and other Asians in Toronto. Such humiliations succeeded in making her, despite her tenured job and success as a writer, "a housebound, fearful, aggrieved, obsessive, and unforgiving queen of bitterness."[7] For a while she tried to combat racism by becoming a civil rights activist. Ultimately, however, she concluded that as long as the Canadian government persisted with its policies on immigration and multiculturalism, she would not be able to make a place for herself and other Indians like her in Canadian society.

To Mukherjee, the United States' melting-pot approach to immigration appeared now to be infinitely better than Canada's stance on multiculturalism, just as immigration now seemed to be much more preferable to expatriation for someone like her, who had decided to uproot herself and wanted desperately to rehouse herself in North America. She therefore moved to the United States, willing herself to think like the immigrants to whom she had once felt superior. She was going to be, she decided, like the countless immigrants before her who had "the will to bond . . . themselves to a new community against the ever-present fear of failure and betrayal" (*Darkness,* 3). It is a decision she has not rued. Indeed, she has allowed a polemical, even uncritical, tone to dominate her writing about immigration, and she now celebrates it and holds it up against expatriation whenever possible.

Mukherjee's life in North America can thus be divided into three phases. At first, she lived the life of an exile in Canada, thinking of herself as an Indian, even as she raised a family and pursued a career in Canada. In the course of her year-long stay in India, however, she discovered that India had become "just another Asian country" (*Days,* 285). Mukherjee then felt ready to commit herself to Canada and embrace the life of an Indian expatriate in that country. But as soon as she perceived that Canada would not accept her as one of its own, she resolved to move to the United States. In the third period of her life in North America, Mukherjee can be seen in a celebratory mood, upholding the life of an immigrant in the United States.

Corresponding to the three phases of her life in North America, Mukherjee's work has gone through three stages. The products of the first phase—*The Tiger's Daughter* and essays she wrote for *Days and Nights in Canada*—are part of the exile's attempt to rethink her connection to India. At the end of her final essays of *Days and Nights in Canada,*

Mukherjee has resolved to shake off her ties to her homeland. The second stage of Mukherjee's writing is made up of *Wife,* most of the stories of *Darkness,* the essay "An Invisible Woman," and the collaborative *The Sorrow and the Terror.* In these works Mukherjee strives to convey directly or indirectly the tensions generated in the Indian expatriate in Canada. Almost all the stories collected in *The Middleman, Jasmine,* and the essays she has been writing recently mark the third stage of her career as a writer of immigrant lives. In this stage her excitement about the possibilities of immigration to the United States, and her view that Asian immigrants to the country can transform themselves there, give her work color and energy.

In *The Holder of the World,* Mukherjee's latest work, she has made a bid to work her Indian heritage into a novel that has also been designed to secure for herself a place in the great tradition of American fiction. Mukherjee now seems to be at that point of her career where she can reconcile her Indianness to her American life and career.

Bharati Mukherjee and Indian Women Immigrants

Not surprisingly, Mukherjee has paid special attention to the condition of the Indian woman immigrant in North America. In her 1990 *Iowa Review* interview she emphasizes that many of her stories are "about psychological transformation, especially among women" immigrants from Asia (15). Asian males, in her view, tend to be too preoccupied about economic transformation to change mentally, and are thus much less interesting as fictional subjects than their wives, who, she avers, run the whole gamut of emotions in their bid to adjust and immerse themselves in a new world. Mukherjee thus writes about women leading lives of quiet desperation, but at least a few of her heroines are shown as women warriors who triumph over the obstacles in their way and who take control over their destinies by crossing cultural lines.

A persistent theme in Mukherjee's later fiction is women refashioning their lives, usually through an encounter with an "other." One can even measure the progress made by Mukherjee's women in their paths to self-realization by looking at the way her novels end: in *Wife* Dimple blunders her way toward liberation by having an affair with a white American man but ends up in madness and suicide; in *Jasmine* the heroine deserts her common-law husband and opts for freedom and an "open" relationship with another white American man; in *The Holder of the World* the narrator, Beigh Masters, as well as the central character, go beyond superficial relationships to a meaningful encounter with Indian men that allow them to be fully themselves.

Mukherjee, however, is no feminist. In fact, she has often been attacked by feminist critics for deviating from their ideals and for making her heroines ultimately cast their lot with men. Her response has been to speak out against "the imperialism" of feminists and to accuse them of being ready to impose "ready-made" solutions to the problems facing immigrant Asian women in North America (1990 interview, 25). She claims that she would much rather show them in the process of acquiring the power that would enable them to control their fates than make them mouthpieces of white, upper-class feminist rhetoric.

Mukherjee's Poetics

Mukherjee's major theme, then, has been the condition of Asian immigrants in North America, particularly the changes taking place in South Asian women in the new world. She has made a conscious effort to make their "intricate and unknowing world comprehensible" to mainstream America through her fiction, and to make Americans aware of the way their continent has been changing because of the stream of Asians who have become their compatriots since the 1960s (1990 interview, 30). Increasingly, Mukherjee has preoccupied herself in showing the impact of America on recent Asian immigrants, but she has also made an effort, especially in her most recent work, to trace the way white Americans have been registering these new Americans in their consciousness.

As befits a practicing novelist who has also been teaching creative writing over two decades, Mukherjee has striven to evolve a poetics that would enable her to articulate her chosen theme. Crucial to her theory of art is her concept of voice, although the concept itself has undergone some changes over the years. Thus in *Days and Nights in Calcutta* Mukherjee has described herself as a writer in search of an "authentic voice," something that would reproduce the life she knew best in a "manner" faithful to her own aesthetic (*Days,* 286). Recently, however, she has talked about finding a "voice" for each work—a "voice" that is the enabling condition of every story and that controls its shape and form. Once she is able to hear such a voice inside her head, the actual writing of a story can take place. This is because voice is "the sum total of every artistic trick" in a writer's bag, controlling her choice of texture, metaphor, point of view, and language. In a sense, the process of capturing the right voice for a story is tantamount to hearing "the main character speak" (1990 interview, 30). To a writer committed to capturing the different and burgeoning Asian immigrant population in America, writing is no longer a search for an "authentic voice" but, rather, a matter of tuning into the tradition of "minority voices, the immigrant voices, the second-generation Jews and Italians and Irish and French-Canadians," that constitute one strand of North American literature.[8]

The task of finding the right voice for a work is obviously related to the work necessary to choose the right point of view from which to tell a story. When she began writing, Mukherjee chose the omniscient point of view and habitually used irony in her work in a conscious bid to distance herself from her heroine. Now that she has dedicated herself to celebrating immigrant voices instead of treating the life of exiles and expatriates with condescension, Mukherjee has tried to minimize the distance between herself and her readers. This has meant that the ironic tone adopted in the earlier works has been replaced by a more intimate perspective.

To Mukherjee, writing is always a conscious, deliberate process. A story may come to her in a flash, but she will revise what she has written carefully, shaping the narrative so that it will please her reader. In *Days and Nights in Calcutta* she describes her "obsessions with opening paragraphs, tone, texture, pacing" and mentions her lectures on creative writing where she emphasizes how fiction is "metaphoric and synecdochic—how every little detail must carry an enormous weight" (253). No matter how obsessive a writer is about her themes, Mukherjee seems to be saying, she must always pay attention to the mechanics of fiction and to language.

As befits a writer with a specific agenda, "the making of new Americans" ("Woman," 26) Mukherjee has paid particular attention to the overall structures of her work. For her, plot is "an arrangement or a design," and she has claimed that "the juxtaposition of images, the composition and framing" are important aspects of her storytelling (1987 interview, 44). Mukherjee's ideal of artistic structure and excellence, she has pointed out, is an Indian Mughal miniature painting where "the corners are as elaborated as the centers" ("Woman," 26). She considers minimalism a limiting trend in contemporary American fiction and eschews the kind of fiction that "exists only in a vacuum of personal relationships"; she would much rather make "a social and political vision . . . an integral part" of her writing and embed her immigrant characters in the thick of American life (1990 interview, 25).

This does not mean, however, that Mukherjee is taking the direct route back to realism. On the contrary, she had made the irrational very much a part of her thematics and has made use of the marvelous in many of her novels and short fiction. As she puts it in the 1987 interview, "My fiction clearly inhabits a space in which there are extra-rational presences" (41). Because she believes the migrants in America go through surprising, even violent, transformations, her novels and short stories are full of startling episodes. She claims that her use of violent incidents is a reflection of what is happening in the American scene but attributes her use of the irrational to her Indian heritage, specifically to the world of Hindu epics, where "shape-changing, miracles, godly perspectives" are common and where characters "transcend the straitjacket of simple psychologizing" ("Woman," 25).

At her best, Mukherjee can combine her commitment to writing fiction that communicates a social and political vision with her belief in a religion that accommodates the marvelous. Her most memorable works reflect her pride in her Indianness but also her decision to celebrate America. In a sense, she is a writer of the Indian diaspora who writes in English, but in another sense she presents immigrant lives in the manner of a Malamud. Certainly, what makes her most worth reading is that part of her aesthetic which wants to make "the familiar exotic, the exotic familiar" ("Woman," 25).

Chapter Two
An Exile's Perspective on "Home"

For a long time, Bharati Mukherjee saw herself in the position of an exile, "someone who inhabits one place and remembers or projects the reality of another."[1] Separated from her family and friends, and all by herself in North America, Mukherjee nourished her memories of her childhood and teens in Calcutta with great care. She felt passionately committed to the city because she felt that the city had shaped her. Letters and newspaper reports about Calcutta and India kept the city and its inhabitants in her mind year after year. Meanwhile, she did graduate studies at the University of Iowa, took up teaching as a career, married, and eventually moved to Canada to take up a tenured position at McGill University. She traveled to Chembur in western India to visit her parents in 1970 but returned to Calcutta only in 1973, taking advantage of a sabbatical to be in the city for almost one year.

Returning to Calcutta after 14 years in North America, she became extracognizant not only of the transformations in the city scene but also of what she recalled of her "home." Calcutta had been changed by years of political violence and economic decline, but she herself had changed so much by her exposure to North American life that her perspective on the city had to alter in this trip. The Calcutta she saw before her seemed unsatisfactory, especially when she recalled the images of it she had cherished in her exile. In some ways, it occurred to her, she could keep alive those images only in voluntary exile. In any case, she decided after her sabbatical year in the city that the life she wanted to live would be available to her only in North America.

Mukherjee's first published novel, *The Tiger's Daughter* (1972), reflects her exilic preoccupation with Calcutta. In this novel, written in Montreal more than a decade after she had left the city, she projects vividly through the experience of her protagonist, an Indian woman called Tara Banerjee Cartwright who is in Calcutta for a visit, the city she remembers. Tara, however, cannot help wondering if it could still be home for her and people of her class, especially since the scenes she had witnessed pointed clearly to the end of their way of life.

The first project on which Mukherjee collaborated with Clark Blaise, a nonfiction work called *Days and Nights in Calcutta* (1977), based on the sabbatical year husband and wife spent in the city and written sometime later, also contains her musings on the place she had long cherished as home. At the end of her contribution to the volume, Mukherjee concludes that there is a wide gap between her and her native place, and that the evolution of her self in exile and her destiny has distanced her irrevocably from the people she had grown up with. Mukherjee has decided that she would henceforth stop thinking of herself as an exile and cast her lot as an individual and as a writer with the countless expatriates who were attempting to make North America their home.

The Tiger's Daughter and Mukherjee's part of *Days and Nights in Calcutta* can thus be considered together. Both works use the motif of the return home from voluntary exile in an alien country and both conclude that expatriation is more desirable than what "home" has become. These works constitute the first phase of Mukherjee's development as a writer and track the initial stage of the route she takes that will bring her eventually to a position from which she can celebrate immigrant lives.

The Tiger's Daughter

In her 1987 *Canadian Fiction Magazine* interview, Mukherjee mentions that *The Tiger's Daughter* was "written on a summer's break in response to a request" from an editor from Houghton Mifflin who had been impressed by a story she had published in *Massachusetts Review* (41). The novel was published on 5 November 1971 and was, on the whole, well received. As Mukherjee puts it in another interview: "*The Tiger's Daughter* was loved by everybody" (1990 interview, 23). Western reviewers singled out for praise the charm, the wit, and the intelligence that were everywhere evident in the novel. John Spurling of the *New Statesman* even compared Mukherjee's first book to *Buddenbrooks* or *The Leopard,* noting that although it was "less grand in scale than either of those books, its tone of voice less ironic than Mann's, less melancholic than Lampedusa's"; it was like those classics in being "a true imaginative explanation of a class in decay rather than a sociological description."[2]

Although Spurling's praise of the novel may be considered excessive, his review does point toward the central themes of *The Tiger's Daughter*: the discovery of the heroine, Tara Banerjee Cartwright, that the city and the people she had come back to be with after years abroad were in a state of terminal decline, her growing awareness of her "foreignness of spirit,"[3] and her eventual realization that her future lay not in it but in expatriation. Spurling evokes Mann and Lampedusa to indicate Mukherjee's affiliations as a novelist in this work, but she herself alludes to Chekhov, T. S. Eliot, and Rupert Brooke to convey the situation facing her heroine. Chekhov, for instance, comes to Tara's mind when she is considering the plight of the upper-class Bengalis of Calcutta, faced with a breakdown of law and order on the one hand and usurpation by the business-minded Marwaris of western India on the other. The helplessness of her friends and family make Tara think of the Russian writer, "yearning for Moscow but staying" (*Daughter,* 45).

The reference to Eliot, significantly, comes at the end of the novel. This time it is not Tara but Joyonto Roy Chowdhury, a Cassandra-like old man whose musings only Tara can value, who remembers fragments from Eliot's "Gerontion"—lines such as, "After such knowledge, what forgiveness?" Like Eliot's character, Joyonto is "An old man in a draughty house / Under a windy knob," waiting for apocalypse, knowing that he was witness to the violent passing of a cycle of Bengali history.

The allusion to Rupert Brooke is also through Joyonto's mind; much earlier in the novel he remembers lines from the poet's "The Soldier" when he sees Tara: "If I should die, think only this of me, / That there's some corner of a foreign field / That is forever." Since this unusual old man, a representative of the high culture associated with the Bengal renaissance, had already singled out Tara as the repository of the values of his class, and since he is preternaturally aware that he himself and those who have chosen to stay back in Calcutta are doomed, the implications of these lines are clear: he will die, but Tara can preserve those values in her life overseas. As he puts it, in another remembered line from another Eliot poem: "Dear Madam, you I shored against my ruins."

Mukherjee manages to present the decay of Calcutta and the decadent life of its upper class with considerable skill. The city seems to be coming apart at its seams because of a number of factors: endemic violence, chronic political unrest, economic stagnation and poverty, disease, overpopulation, and class conflicts. The opening-page description of the street scene outside the Catelli-Continental, a luxury hotel that was once one of the glories of Calcutta, is indicative of the extent of the city's decline: the entrance now seems "small, almost shabby," the walls "are patterned with rust and mold," the "sidewalks along the hotel are painted with obscenities and political slogans" (*Daughter,* 3). On them are "a colony of beggars" and "shriveled women" selling their wares. And yet the hotel could once be described as "the navel of the universe," for there was a time when Calcutta was *the* imperial city of British India, the center of commercial and political power, and the hotel the place where powerful people would assemble for tea and talk. Now the Calcutta elite still met here and went through "their daily ritual of espresso or tea" (*Daughter,* 4), but they were people who talked without conviction and were increasingly under siege from people full of passionate intensity, ready to mob and brutalize them.

And yet the Calcutta beau monde acted as if "the real Calcutta, the thick laughter of brutal men, open dustbins, warm and dark where carcasses were sometimes discarded, did not exist" (*Daughter,* 41). Or if they did admit that "everything's gone down horribly" (*Daughter,* 42), they were not ready to do anything to change the situation, having little appetite for heroic gestures. Their tendency was to talk about moving out, or to slide into inaction, or to strike a pose of mock horror or indifference. A couplet from a W. H. Davies poem, quoted in the middle of a picnic arranged in Tara's honor, sums up perfectly the fin de siècle atmosphere of upper-class Calcutta evoked by Mukherjee in her novel: "What is this life, if full of care, / We have no time to stand and stare." Events such as the picnic served to assuage "their sense of panic, their racial and class fears," and allowed them to reconstruct another Calcutta, "one they longed to return to, more stable, less bitter" (*Daughter,* 98).

Nostalgia or insouciance appear to be the only alternatives available to Tara's friends; after some time in the city even Tara begins to feel "that the misery of her city was too immense and blurred to be listed and assailed one by one. That it was fatal to fight for justice; that it was better to remain passive and absorb all shocks as they came" (*Daughter,* 131). After successive characters describe Calcutta as hell on earth, Tara herself begins to think that despite the few pleasant moments she has had in the city in this trip home, "Calcutta was the deadliest city in the world; alarm and impatience were equally useless" (*Daughter,* 168). No wonder, then, that Tara's husband, David Cartwright, reading her reports about the city as well as the *New Yorker*'s Ved Mehta's journals on India, concludes that Calcutta was "the collective future in which garbage, disease, and stagnation are man's estate."

In her 1987 *Canadian Fiction Magazine* interview, Mukherjee, just after observing that her novel dealt with "the violent passing of an era," comments that "the characters were intended to be fleshed out abstractions" (41). In Mukherjee's scheme of things, Tara's friends are, as Joyonto Roy Chowdhury puts it, "trapped gazelles," although apparently "confident, handsome and brashly opinionated" (*Daughter,* 41). It is easy to see that Joyonto himself is "a dying savior" (*Daughter,* 83), a prophet unheeded by everyone in the novel except Tara, who at the end of the novel will hear his message of doom and his admonition to her to leave. Another abstraction, not fleshed out in the novel as are Tara's friends and Joyonto, but given a representative significance, is Deepak Ghose. Not a character who plays a part in the action of the novel but merely a name noticed by Tara in posters printed by a Marxist party, he is significant because he indicates that one possible fate that can overtake Calcutta is revolution.

But the character who seems most likely to seize the situation in Calcutta and use it to his advantage is the Marwari businessman-politician P. K. Tuntunwala. When Tara first meets him on the train from Bombay to Calcutta she is reminded by him of "a circus animal who had gotten the better of his master" (*Daughter,* 20). Imaged variously as a spider, a monkey, and a shark, he is the classic usurper, a captain of industry and a leader from a community of businessmen who had taken over Calcutta commerce. Marwaris like him were steadily displacing the old wealth represented by someone such as Joyonto Roy Chowdhury, whose financial strength came from landed property. Driven by self-interest, and a creature of immense energy, he is seemingly about to grab political power in Calcutta, too, by presenting himself as the law-and-order candidate. It occurs to Tara at one point that he is "a dangerous man. He could create whatever situation, whatever catastrophe he needed" (*Daughter,* 77). Although Tara is initially repelled by him, and although he is loud in his proclamation that he had no time for "heart's matters [which] are for idiots and women" (*Daughter,* 132), she soon finds herself attracted to a man of such obvious energy and determination, fascinated by what, in another context, she would have perceived as an abomination. Like her journalist friend Sanjay, she is taken in by this poseur's message: "strength is love" (*Daughter,* 133).

Next to Tuntunwala, the typical Bengali businessman, represented in the novel by Tara's friend Pronob, appears effete and ineffectual. In Tara's eyes, the Marwari was "a man of such energy, so aggressive, so brittle and ferocious," that beside him "Pronob seemed flabby" (*Daughter,* 134). Another figure from the business world with whom Tuntunwala can be compared is Tara's father, popularly known as "the Bengal Tiger" for his business prowess. But for all his strength and courage, even her father cannot save Tara from becoming Tuntunwala's victim. Significantly, when Tara thinks of Tuntunwala and Pronob, she also thinks of her father, but her thoughts only make her want to cry. Significantly, also, her father is away when Tuntunwala makes his move to molest Tara, and Tuntunwala warms up to this move by boasting to her of a tiger he has shot and by expressing his desire to show her "the selfsame tiger skin" in his house one day (*Daughter,* 194). Mukherjee's point here seems to be that even tough-minded Bengali industrialists like her father are too simple for the times and less compelling than the brutal figures who would now impose their wills over Calcutta life.

In fact, Tara's father is of the same Bengali patrician class that produced someone like Joyonto and that is in danger of being overthrown by left-wing revolutionaries such as Deepak Ghose or right-wing marauders such as Tuntunwala. *The Tiger's Daughter* presents the history as well as the life of this class with care. The novel thus contains episodes from earlier Bengali social history and shows readers glimpses of a more graceful and ordered Calcutta. But though we get to read about such glorious episodes of Bengali history as the anticolonial *swadeshi* movement remembered by Joyonto, everywhere history is in retreat and the old landmarks of Calcutta culture are being replaced. For example, the city's fashionable Park Street district has just witnessed the opening of the small but smart Kapoor's Restaurant, "the symbol of modern India" that had "marked the end of tea shops like Arioli's and Chandler's," where European ladies would once snack (*Daughter,* 83). Semi-feudal Bengal, idealistic Bengalis, and the colonial city stand little chance of surviving the violence of revolutionaries, the cunning of conservative politicians, upheavals in the economy, and the violent winds of change.

In the course of the novel, then, Tara must come to terms with the new Calcutta and must come to realize that the images of the city she had preserved in her memory in North America no longer correspond to the city scenes she was now viewing on her trip home. As she finds out: "except for Camac Street [where her parents lived], Calcutta had changed greatly; and even Camac Street had felt the first stirring of death" (*Daughter,* 199). Mukherjee presents the novel through an omniscient narrator, but the reader sees things mostly from Tara's point of view; she is the third-person center-of-consciousness through whom Mukherjee registers her disenchantment with the changes that have taken place in Calcutta.

As Maya Manju Sharma points out in "The Inner World of Bharati Mukherjee: From Expatriate to Immigrant," "that Tara is the alter ego of the author is clear from the autobiographical details in *Days and Nights*; the testings of Tara are also battles in the growth of the author's sensibility from that of the expatriate to that of the immigrant."[4] Like Mukherjee, Tara has married a North American novelist who prefers to stay back during his summer breaks so that he can write; like her creator, Tara was overcome by bouts of homesickness when in North America and returns to Calcutta to gauge the extent of her commitment to what was once home.

Mukherjee, however, has denied that the novel is "based on any real person" and has declared that "the novel wasn't autobiographical" (1987 interview, 41). One difference between her and Tara, she hints, is Tara's passivity, a trait "dictated by her dramatic function in the novel" and the reason that she can be molested by someone like Tuntunwala. According to Mukherjee, Tara "had to be porous and passive in order to record the slightest tremors in her culture. She had to react rather than act" (1987 interview, 41). Certainly, Tara's passivity makes her the perfect instrument for recording the discordant aspects of contemporary Calcutta; because she cannot say "no" she will go out not only with the repellent Tuntunwala to see his new industrial estate but also with the enigmatic Joyonto to view the slums that are being built on the old man's property. Observant, sensitive, vulnerable, and not a little confused, she moves in and out of different social orbits and in the process makes them available for our scrutiny.

The seven years she has spent in the West has inevitably altered Tara's angle of vision. As she drives past Bombay's Marine Drive on her way back to Calcutta, she finds the street to be "run-down and crowded," and yet seven years earlier she had "admired" the place and found it "fashionable" (*Daughter,* 18). When she was in North America she could not stop thinking of home, but now in this trip to Calcutta she misses David and fears losing him continually. She remembers even now the sense of alienation she had in New York but cannot cease ruminating in Calcutta on "the foreignness of spirit" she was experiencing in the city of her birth (*Daughter,* 37). She spends a lot of time in Calcutta with her upper-class Bengali friends, recognizing that they were "shavings of her personality," and yet cannot help fearing "their tone, their omissions, their aristocratic oneness" (*Daughter,* 43). She may react "guiltily" to her friend Pronob's comment that he would "hate to be a nobody in America" (*Daughter,* 59) but has the distinct feeling on a number of occasions in India that to at least a few of her friends and family she is now, quite literally, an outcast because of her marriage to a white North American. On other occasions, however, she herself feels "quite cut off" from the people she grew up with (*Daughter,* 89). It does not take her very long to feel that depression is overcoming her, and she begins to think that it is best to return to New York.

What Tara had not known before coming to Calcutta but must discover is what is obvious to her friend Reena. As Reena puts it in her Indian-English idiom, "You've changed too much, Tara" (*Daughter*, 105). She begins to let "little things . . . upset her" and comes to realize that "of late she had been outraged by Calcutta." Even the language she had used so spontaneously once upon a time now appears strange: "she had forgotten so many Indian-English words she had once used with her friends" (*Daughter*, 107). Again and again, she finds herself reacting to an event very differently from them. What surprises or shocks her in Calcutta appears to be quite routine to someone like Reena. Similarly, what she considers sensible and decorous seems silly and outrageous to others. For instance, her suggestion that women participating in a beauty contest should wear swimsuits leads to this rebuke from an Indian physician: "I think your years abroad have robbed you of feminine propriety or you are joking with us" (*Daughter*, 187).

The Tiger's Daughter, then, is designed to capture the predicament of someone returning to her homeland after a period of self-imposed exile: to such a person, home will never be home again, and life in exile, bitter draught though it often is, will be preferable to what home has become. The discovery that Tara makes at the end of the novel is that the greenery and the forests she had associated with the India of her childhood— her version of pastoral—were no longer there, something or the other had "killed" them (*Daughter*, 207). In New York she had dreamed of coming back to Calcutta, but "the return had brought only wounds" (*Daughter*, 25). Particularly galling for Tara is her finding that by choosing exile she "had slipped outside" the parameters of a world in which she belonged by birthright, and that even after only seven years outside it, "reentry was barred" (*Daughter*, 110). And so although the novel ends with Tara trapped in a car that is surrounded by rioters, wondering "whether she would ever get out of Calcutta, and if she didn't, whether David would ever know that she loved him fiercely" (*Daughter*, 210), Tara's mental progress in the novel leaves no doubt in the reader's mind that if she did get out of the car, it would be to take the next plane back to the United States.

Although David does not take part in any of the events described in the novel, Mukherjee uses him skillfully to comment on the problems inherent in a cross-cultural relationship. He is also the implied reader of the novel, a liberal North American who reads about Tara's experience of

Calcutta with some interest but also with a measure of incomprehension. Tara often wonders about the difficulties of communicating her feelings about her city and its people to David. For instance, while imagining the indignities her Calcutta friends were having to endure then, she cannot help thinking, "How could she explain the bitterness of it to David, who would have laughed at her friends and wished them luck as refugees?" (*Daughter,* 45). How could she explain to David who was, after all, "a foreigner" (*Daughter,* 48), her mother's obsession with insurance policies? Just as she could not explain to her Calcutta friends why there were ghettos and student demonstrations in New York—they persisted in believing that "America was lovely" and that "New York was not like Calcutta" (*Daughter,* 56)—she could not explain to David, who "was hostile to genealogies and had often misunderstood her affection for the family as overdependence" (*Daughter,* 64), the Indian's emotional stake in the notion of the extended family. Because he is secure in his world of stable identities and predictable events, Tara feels that she cannot confide in David some things about her vacation in Calcutta, for he "expected everything to have some meaning or point" (*Daughter,* 130), whereas she was experiencing so much that was chaotic or formless or incomprehensible. She knew thus that David would react to "the misery" of her city with "outrage" and a plan for quick and decisive action, but how would he understand that the problems of Calcutta were "too immense and blurred to be listed and assailed one by one" (*Daughter,* 131)?

Misunderstanding, confusion, and incomprehension, then, are inevitable in any cross-cultural encounter. Passages to and out of India, Mukherjee appears to be saying, will cause pain and bewilderment. There are limits not only to David's understanding of and tolerance for Indians, but also to India's ability to accept or comprehend someone like Tara's husband. Two memorable minor characters of *The Tiger's Daughter*—Washington McDowell and Antonia Whitehead—illustrate the extent of the confusion created in the contact zones between cultures. McDowell is an American student who comes to Calcutta on an exchange program and who is supposed to stay with Reena's family when in the city. They look forward to his visit with great excitement but then are shocked to discover that they would be hosting a black American. Shock gives way to dismay for Reena's mother when she begins to suspect her daughter of having an affair with an "African" (*Daughter,* 138). But McDowell turns out to be a Black Panther who soon deserts his affluent hosts to take up the cause of Calcutta's revolutionaries.

Antonia Whitehead, a big redheaded American out on a "mission" to save the Third World, bumbles her way through India and occasions this impassioned editorial from Tara's journalist friend Sanjay: "It has been said that she is really a blessing in disguise, that she is a missionary defrocked, that she is Deepak Ghose's special lady friend. But I say . . . she is dangerous" (*Daughter,* 164–65). Although Tara knows that Antonia is just as she was in her first few weeks in this trip home— "impatient, menacing and equally innocent" (*Daughter,* 166)—she is aware that the white American girl was destined to create much confusion during her stay in India. But because Tara has learned earlier that "it was impossible to be a bridge for anyone" since "bridges had a way of cluttering up the landscape" (*Daughter,* 144), she lets Antonia blunder her way through India and be misconstrued by the Indians with whom she comes in contact.

By suggesting the difficulties of passages in and out of India and by pointing at bridges that cannot be built between cultures, Mukherjee is, of course, alluding to E. M. Forster's classic novel. Mukherjee has acknowledged in her interviews that she had set out in her first novel to deliberately mimic and subvert *A Passage to India*. She has revealed that the swimming pool scene of her novel is based on Forster's Mau tank episode—only in *The Tiger's Daughter* there is no "regeneration" to be had from the swimming pool since ennui will continue to be the dominant emotion of its users (1990 interview, 24). Mukherjee has also noted that her novel has "a rather British feel to it," because of her use of the omniscient point of view and irony in the manner of Jane Austen, Dickens, and Forster. Her "comic vision," she feels, puts *The Tiger's Daughter* in the British tradition, for "most of the characters, even when they are caught in ghastly situations, acquaint themselves in amusing ways" (1987 interview, 43). Another scene that appears to echo an episode from Forster is Tara's visit to the slum that has grown up on Joyonto's estate, for when Tara looses her composure because a little girl with sores on her legs screams at her she is reacting just as Adela Quested did in the Marabar Cave episode of Forster's novel.

In general, it can be said that Mukherjee handles the various Calcutta settings of *The Tiger's Daughter* dexterously. Her characters may be "fleshed out abstractions" (1987 interview, 43), but her descriptions of Calcutta scenes are quite realistic, as is the episode set in the west Bengal hill station of Darjeeling. Mukherjee's first novel also reveals that she has a good ear for dialogue, and her use of Indian-English idioms is particularly effective. The novel benefits, too, from a tightly knit structure. It thus ends as it began—just outside the Catelli-Continental Hotel. In the concluding chapter, however, this hotel, once the symbol of Calcutta's preeminence in India but already decrepit in the opening episode, is under siege, and we know that the novel has charted a further step downwards in the city's fortunes. Some scenes also stand out because of Mukherjee's ability to depict complicated emotions that are barely under control and her skill in representing the sparks that are set off when tense people interact. A good example of such a scene is Tara's visit to her long-suffering Aunt Jharna—a visit that climaxes quickly when the older woman flares up at Tara's suggestion that her handicapped daughter try plaster casts and special shoes.

Aunt Jharna's quietly violent response to Tara's innocuous suggestion can be seen as a paradigm of the response many Indian critics have had to this and other Mukherjee books on India and Indians. Aunt Jharna rebukes Tara thus: "You've come back to make fun of us, haven't you? What gives you the right? Your American money? Your *mleccha* [outcast] husband?" (*Daughter*, 36). Many readers have similarly been outraged by Mukherjee's diagnosis of the malaise afflicting Calcutta and have seen scant sympathy, more than a touch of malice, and not a little condescension in her depiction of Calcutta and its people. In " 'In the Presence of History': The Representation of Past and Present Indias in Bharati Mukherjee's Fiction," Debjani Banerjee has accused the novelist of "the uniformly negative portrayal of the political movement" that was so important to many Bengalis in the 1960s and 1970s.[5] In this critic's view, Mukherjee's lack of sympathy for the movement, like Tara's "consistent othering of MacDowell," is an assertion of the "inflexibility of difference which makes communication impossible across categories of gender, class, and race." Banerjee even sees in the novelist's slighting treatment of the movement threatening the Calcutta elites to which she belonged a "paranoia" that is "largely exaggerated and misplaced." It is also Banerjee's contention that parts of the novel seem to be deliberately constructed to take the novel's upper-class Indian and Western readers on a guided tour of Calcutta's problem areas. Even the unattributed review of the novel published in the *Times Literary Supplement* indicts Mukherjee for her ironic and unsympathetic treatment of contemporary Calcutta and nostalgia for the past and notes that such treatment makes *The Tiger's Daughter* "charming and intelligent—and curiously unmoving."[6]

Nevertheless, Mukherjee's first novel is an impressive achievement. It announces a bold new voice in literature in English coming out of India to represent the predicament of the Indian who has opted to settle in the West and must now redefine her ties to her homeland. *The Tiger's Daughter* and *Days and Nights in Calcutta,* her next work, are the books Mukherjee had to write before she could sever her ties with the country of her birth and cast her lot with countless expatriates in North America to come to the point from where she could ultimately celebrate immigrant lives and immigration to the United States.

Days and Nights in Calcutta

At one point in *The Tiger's Daughter* Mukherjee's heroine, Tara, wonders how her husband, David, would react to Calcutta. Tara cannot see David as the average American tourist—camera slung on his shoulder, photographing the obvious features of the city. David, she knows, would not want to "capture in color the pain of Calcutta" (*Daughter,* 108), but she thinks that it is possible that "he would analyze her life and her friends in the lens of his Minolta." But she concludes in the end that the only thing that could be said with certainty about David was that he would try to "see the real India."

Tara's thoughts about her husband's response to Calcutta are interesting, especially when viewed in the context of *Days and Nights in Calcutta*. This unique work, the product of the sabbatical year that Mukherjee and Clark Blaise spent in India in 1973–74, juxtaposes the perspectives of this writing couple and suggests in the process what David really would have seen in the Indian city. But while Blaise does manage to record something of the "real India" Tara knew her husband would capture, the collaborative work assumes special significance when considered as an indispensable part of Mukherjee's oeuvre and integral to her developing vision of her status as an expatriate writer.

It was Blaise's idea that he and Mukherjee keep separate journals of the months they would spend in Calcutta so that they could later publish them under one cover as *The Bengal Journals*. The book, they felt at that time, would be "simply the record of a day-to-day account of two people going to India" (1990 interview, 15). Husband and wife continued to work on their journals when they went back to their jobs in Montreal and when they passed some more time in India in 1976 and 1977. Their contract with Doubleday & Company specified that they refrain from sharing their experiences or exchanging notes while writing the journals. It was only after they had completed their writing, therefore, that they and their editors decided on an alternate chapter format for their project.

What must have struck wife and husband as they compared their work was how different and yet complementary their records of their year in India had turned out to be. Blaise's section reflects clearly the response of a man who "want[s] to understand it all" and who is "benevolently disposed towards everything" he comes across in his Indian trip (*Days,* 14). But Blaise's attempt to evaluate his experience of India is motivated at least in part by a personal goal. As he comes to realize, "My quest was nothing less than the retrieval of a buried self, the understanding of my marriage" (*Days,* 84). Visiting India would enable him to appreciate the forces that had gone into the making of his wife, thereby strengthening his marriage.

Blaise's chapters of *Days and Nights in Calcutta* thus consist of a series of impressions of India and of Mukherjee's family and friends. He tries to take in everything that he comes across. Street scenes, servants, social rituals, urban settings, intellectual life, his father-in-law at work or at prayer, and the Indian joint family are only some of his concerns. The persona the reader comes across in his section of the book is engaging and enthusiastic, well-meaning and even a little wide-eyed. Only occasionally does he irritate by revealing a penchant for generalizing or essentializing India or by being self-consciously literary. For example, while ruminating on the Air-India building in Bombay, he writes, "For a Westerner, there is enough unknown even on the steps of the Air-India Building, or with friends and family, especially on the streets of any Indian city, to satisfy all his tastes for texture and design" (*Days,* 19). But his obvious delight in his subjects redeems his narrative as does his sincerity in trying to make up for 10 years of married life, when he had been content "in knowing Bharati on my own terms and in my language" (*Days,* 96).

Mukherjee's chapters of *Days and Nights in Calcutta* concentrate mostly on the lives of the upper-middle-class women of the city with whom she had gone to school and on her discovery that there was a gulf that separated her now from them. She seemed to have set out to write a book about these women and some of the other people she met during her stay but "ended up writing . . . an accidental autobiography" (1987 interview, 36). Writing the book traumatized her, for as she came to terms with the year she had spent in Calcutta she realized that "for all the trouble I was going through in Canada, it was still the new world that I wanted to live in, and that the old world was dead for me" (1990 interview, 15). Mukherjee's section of *Days and Nights in Calcutta* turns on this discovery and is thus a much more intense account than Blaise's of their trip to the city.

Initially, however, it had appeared to Mukherjee that not much had changed in Calcutta, just as her relations kept telling her when they first met her that despite her Canadian husband and children she hadn't changed much either. Ballygunge, the neighborhood in which she had spent the first few years of her life in a joint family situation, seemed to be more or less as she had remembered it. But as she finds out, some things had changed. It occurs to Mukherjee, for instance, that the joint family system was on the verge of collapse. Mukherjee sees in the Calcutta that she comes back to in 1973 "the impulse to erect compound walls, to isolate and exclude" (*Days,* 185). With the Naxalite revolution just behind them, Calcutta's upper class had become much more security conscious. As Veena, one of Mukherjee's friends, points out in response to Mukherjee's automatic comment that Calcutta had not really changed, the city "has changed," only their class pretended that it had not to make things easier for themselves (*Days,* 207). Rich or poor, Calcuttans had become obsessed with the idea of survival. The economic and political situation was getting worse, and nothing could be taken for granted anymore. Even a visit to the exclusive Calcutta Turf Club on a beautiful day can turn without warning into an encounter with a mob, ready to riot and destroy.

In the beginning it appeared to Mukherjee that her convent-school friends were leading perfectly happy lives. One of them even expresses her regret at the events that had removed Mukherjee "so far from the comforting, circumscribed life" which they lived in Calcutta (*Days,* 200). All of them seemed to agree on one point: they would not live anywhere else and were committed to Calcutta. But Mukherjee also hears them talk of the hard times that were just ahead and the importance of getting ready for "the crises that now seemed unavoidable" (*Days,* 203). As she came closer to her friends and began to probe deeper into their lives, she detected in them "deep and bizarre passions that kept them confined to a city which had begun to act toward them with the maliciousness of a bitter dying relative" (*Days,* 204).

Mukherjee devotes considerable space in her part of *Days and Nights in Calcutta* to individual case studies of the lives of a few upper- and upper-middle-class women of the city. Veena, for example, looked serene in her luxurious house but talked to her in a candid moment of her experience of class warfare. Anjali, with whom Mukherjee had once been particularly close, tells her that their way of life was dying and allows her to see that the society that she "had assumed was marvelously elastic and open and friendly" was also "simultaneously rigid, hierarchical, and exclusive" (*Days,* 212). On the surface, a woman like Anjali was content and played perfectly the roles required of her by her society: she was the ideal wife, mother, mistress of her household servants, and patron of the city's poor. But like the Sita of Hindu myths, Anjali and other women like her had sacrificed themselves for their husbands; they were essentially women who "had never stopped self-expurgating" (*Days,* 214). Another acquaintance Mukherjee remembers from her school days for carrying off innumerable prizes and for wanting to be a top-flight lawyer had now become a hard and abrasive woman who complained of predetermined lives. Getting to know these women again after 14 years, Mukherjee concludes that something was "terribly, terribly wrong" with the world she was now reentering and that "what is unforgivable is the lives that have been sacrificed to notions of propriety and obedience" (*Days,* 217).

Mukherjee finds the case of Meena, the wife of a rich Marwari businessman, particularly galling. Even though her husband had studied in the United States, Meena is having to struggle with their community's code that dictates that a woman should not study because "education gets in the way of husband worship" (*Days,* 266). Determined to defy her in-laws and to become a writer, Meena knows she might have to do something drastic to break out of the mold made for Marwari women. Mukherjee records that Meena's story had made her cry and made her angry and that that anger even shaped her second novel, *Wife,* where the protagonist cannot contain her violent feelings against her husband and ends up killing him.

In "Bharati Mukherjee as Autobiographer," the only essay-length analysis of *Days and Nights in Calcutta* published till now, Pramila Venkateswaran notes how Meena's story reveals "the pockets of anger rumbling beneath the surface calm" and sees Meena as "symbolic of the resistance and rebellion threatening to challenge a crippling tradition."[7] Venkateswaran goes on to declare that while the women whose stories Mukherjee has compiled in her book have let themselves be constricted by a tradition that directs them toward self-sacrifice, there is also a tradition of female self-empowerment through suffering and sacrifice in Hinduism that Mukherjee downplays. In Venkateswaran's view, Mukherjee has become too conscious of her difference from the women

she meets in the sabbatical year in Calcutta and too committed to immigration to be fair to this tradition of resistance. Venkateswaran believes
that Mukherjee offers the various case histories documented in her book
mainly to counterpoint them to her own rediscovery of her identity as a
woman and a writer dedicated to immigrant lives.

It is important to remember, however, that Mukherjee begins her
account of her Indian trip by describing her alienation and sense of exhaustion in Canada. She describes how she had felt a sense of isolation in
Canada's vastness and how she was tired of being treated as an exotic or as
the wife of a famous Canadian writer there. Also, in the space of a few
months, he broke a hand, they lost their house in a fire, and she received
injuries in a car accident. Traumatized, they decided to use the money they
had collected from their insurance claims to go on a long vacation to a
place where they could be free from stress. Spending their sabbatical year
in Calcutta was Blaise's idea, but Mukherjee embraced it eagerly because
she felt she could control her destiny better in the city of her birth.

But if Mukherjee believed that she would be accepted easily by
Calcutta or that reentry into the world she had left behind would pose
no problem, she was soon disabused of such notions. Even her husband
could see that their diasporic moves had made the Mukherjee girls lose
"their place in the joint family that is India" (*Days,* 57) and that his wife
in particular had become "an outsider because of her marriage, her residence, and especially her choice of English as an artistic language" (*Days,*
115).[8] When Mukherjee is upset by her discovery on the plane from
Bombay to Calcutta of a hair in the snack that had been served to her,
the man in the next seat is sure of her status: she must be "a resident
alien" in Canada because Indians had learned not to let such little things
bother them (*Days,* 198). The incident pains her, for it amounts to a discovery even before she lands in Calcutta that her connections to Canada
were only too obvious. Mukherjee had apprehended before coming to
India that her "Indianness is fragile" and that her "decades-long use of
English as a first language had cut" her off from her country (*Days,* 170);
what she was not prepared for was the extent of the divide separating
her from India because of this and other aspects of her exile's experience.

Talking to her mother in Chembur on the first night of their holiday
in India, Mukherjee becomes conscious again about the distance she had
traveled in leaving India and settling down in Canada. Her mother tells
her that she had premonitions of the danger her daughter had been in in
Canada and had reached her there at those times through mental telepathy, but such talk makes Mukherjee distinctly uncomfortable. Life in

exile, she implies, inevitably eroded her faith in magic or telepathy. Mukherjee remembers now how even the five years she passed with her parents and sisters in England when she was growing up had changed her, causing her to view herself differently, to bend her personality, and to relinquish her roots.

Although Mukherjee tries to reroot herself in Calcutta by immersing herself in the social life of the city, everywhere she goes and everything that she observes reminds her of her alienation from Calcuttans. What especially bothers her is that while she cannot connect herself to the life of the city and has to agonize over most things, most of her friends managed to "preserve their innocence in the midst of city-wide misery without any morbid inward-turning" (*Days,* 205). Participating with her friends in a charity project to assist lepers, she observes how dedicated they were to their work and how they had personalized the problem of the lepers while she could only worry about the nature of the satisfaction they got from such work. In one memorable episode where one of her friends' husband whimsically forces a madwoman to dance in the streets after midnight and harasses a poor rickshaw-puller just to have some fun at these two people's expense, Mukherjee realizes that she had done well to curb her impulse to stop the tomfoolery that she was having to witness. She might have been "not innocent enough to enjoy it" and "not wise enough to discriminate between malice and play," but everyone else present "had all known their roles" (*Days,* 251).

In fact, Mukherjee comes to realize that despite her efforts to reconnect herself with her friends and family, they will no longer accept her within their midst without reservation. In Montreal she knew that others saw her as "a brown woman in a white society, different, perhaps even special, but definitely not a part of the majority" (*Days,* 179), but in Calcutta she is "an intimidating alien" to even her female relatives because of the way she argued in her American accent with "male relatives about tax breaks and inflation" and the way she was not prepared to defer to men they considered holy (*Days,* 225). When she is out in the streets with Blaise she knows that she is perceived as "the Indian memsahib with a white escort to be lewdly stared at, or to be whispered 'good day' to by elevator-boy-pimps" (*Days,* 239). And when she is out all by herself, she cannot help projecting a "foreign image" even to domestic servants (*Days,* 252). At times she even feels that she is considered by some people in Calcutta to be a little bizarre.

Not surprisingly, there were moments in the year she and Blaise spent in Calcutta when she did feel that she had been readmitted to the world she had left behind and when she began to think once more like an inhabitant of the city. At such moments she would cast aside some of the liberal notions she had imbibed in the West and would look down on the self-centered life she had been leading in Montreal. There were times, too, when she would feel completely at home in Calcutta and not "as exposed, as helplessly foreign" as she did in Montreal (*Days,* 206).

Nevertheless, such moments were few and far between, and most of the time Mukherjee records her sense of having become something other than what she had once been in Calcutta and someone different from the people she was now meeting in the city. Indeed, Mukherjee becomes aware as her year in Calcutta progresses that for her "it was a time to subvert memory, to hunt down sly conciliatory impulses" (*Days,* 221). Thus, at the end of the year spent in the city of her birth, Mukherjee declares she was glad to leave India and ready to view herself henceforth as an immigrant and not as an exile. She had made friends in Calcutta in the months she had been there and had enjoyed being "racially invisible," but India would no longer be for her "a talisman" that would enable her to survive as an exile in Canada (*Days,* 284). From now on her memories of India would be like the ghost of her uncle which visits her in Chembur in the last phase of their trip—a familiar compound ghost, a specter that haunted her once in a while without unsettling her in any way. With this trip to India she had crossed her Rubicon; from now on it would be for her "just another Asian country," and she would be in it only as "another knowledgeable but desolate tourist" (*Days,* 285).

It is at this point of her part of *Days and Nights in Calcutta* that Mukherjee comes to a conclusion that will be absolutely crucial to the next phase of her poetics: from now on she would stop thinking of herself as an Indian woman writer living in self-imposed exile in the West and would have to write as an expatriate writer. There would be no more going back for her to India as the sole setting of her fiction and no longer would she attempt to create a "Chekhovian image of India" (*Days,* 285) as she had in her first novel. She would have to find her own voice, although she could model it on V. S. Naipaul, another "accidental tourist" who "has written most movingly about the pain and absurdity of art and exile, of 'Third World art' and exile among the former colonizers; the tolerant incomprehension of hosts, the absolute impossibility of ever having a home" (*Days,* 287). That part of her which had wanted to be consoled for being an exile had died in the course of the days and nights she had been through in India, but she had been impressed at the

end of her sabbatical year with her spirit of resilience, which urged her to
go on to be an artificer of expatriation.

In the concluding paragraph of her portion of *Days and Nights in
Calcutta,* Mukherjee attempts to unite the two subjects she had been
counterpointing throughout her narrative: the lot of Indian women and
the developing vision of her own self. Although she has abandoned the
role reserved for women of her class, she will have the strength to go on
because she is an Indian woman who has, typically, "a secretive love of
revengeful survival" (*Days,* 287). Pramila Venkateswaran, therefore, is
not being completely fair to Mukherjee when she observes that
Mukherjee does not take notice of the tradition in which Indian women
discover that their experience of suffering can make them powerful. It is
true, of course, that Mukherjee herself has been too privileged almost all
her life to have undergone anything like the sufferings of the Calcutta
women she had herself documented in her book, but she would like us to
believe that her knowledge of what these women were going through
does enable her to strike out in a different direction and ultimately
empower her as an artist. Venkateswaran, however, is right in identifying
what is unique about *Days and Nights in Calcutta*: it is a work "created at
the intersection of cultures, of postcolonial and 'free' worlds, of 'tradition' and 'modernity', of East and West"; it "occupies the indeterminate
area between self-portraiture and journalistic reportage, between self-
writing and cultural anamnesis" (Venkateswaran, 23). It is also the book
Mukherjee had to write to discover that what she wanted really to be
was a writer not writing about exiles but about expatriates and immigrants.

Chapter Three
The Aloofness of Expatriation

The sabbatical year that Bharati Mukherjee spent in India in 1973 had convinced her that henceforth she would have to view herself not as an Indian in self-imposed exile in Canada but as a North American, and that the condition of expatriation was what she would have to embrace in the future as the major theme of her art. Mukherjee felt sure now that there was no point for her anymore to hold on to the happy memories of her Indian years as a "talisman against icy Canada" (*Days*, 285), and that she could compensate herself for the condition of exile by the gains to be had from following such an author as V. S. Naipaul, who wrote "most movingly about the pain and absurdity of art and exile, of 'Third World art' and exile among the former colonizers; the tolerant incomprehension of hosts, the impossibility of ever having a home, a *desh*" (*Days*, 287). In other words, she would have to move beyond India as a setting and consider themes other than the clash of cultures in the sub-continent; the time had come for her, she felt at this point of her writing career, to cast her gaze on the lot of Indian expatriates in the New World and "to astonish, even shock" (*Days*, 287) her Western readers with narratives of the new immigrants in their midst.

But if Mukherjee was ready by 1974 to embrace expatriation and think of Canada as the country that represented the future for her and her family, she was not prepared for the prejudice against South Asians and the indifference her work met in that country. In her prize-winning and hard-hitting essay "An Invisible Woman," Mukherjee explains with some passion and considerable indignation how her dreams of settling in Canada and carving a place for herself in the country's cultural life was shattered by her experience of racism and insularity in Montreal and Toronto. Mukherjee describes the many humiliations she suffered in public because of her racial origins, of harassment suffered at the hands of customs officials who questioned her right to be in Canada, or of private detectives in hotels and department stores who suspected her of unlawful entry into their domains. Unnerved by questions flung at her such as "Why don't you go back to Africa?" or of taunts and snubs from unemployed or lower-class Canadians resentful of Asians who seemed to them to be flocking in to snatch away jobs and government handouts, Mukherjee was also unsettled by an official policy of "multiculturalism" that seemingly relegated her and her kind to a second-class existence and made a point of underlining the exotic nature of South Asian immigrants.

But it is not only the uncultured Canadian or the bureaucratic government official whom Mukherjee faults in her essay for marginalizing her and traumatizing her; she makes the entire Canadian cultural establishment guilty of rendering her invisible and of not wanting her to belong. Thus, she points out that in Canada she was more or less ignored as a writer; despite the good reviews garnered by *The Tiger's Daughter,* she was not invited to give readings or join the Writer's Union of Canada. As far as Mukherjee was concerned, "multiculturalism" was essentially an excuse for not allowing other cultures to merge with the dominant culture and to keep new immigrants like her outside mainstream Canada.

As a result of the hostility she felt she had to fend off all the time and of the deliberate policy of neglect she thought was being pursued by Canada's cultural establishment, Mukherjee found herself leading two lives in the country: one part of her felt secure as "a full professor at McGill, an author, a confident lecturer," but another life she was leading simultaneously was that of "a house-bound, aggrieved, obsessive, and unforgiving queen of bitterness" ("Invisible," 39). In this mood, she reacted with a shock of recognition to stories of "men going berserk, or women committing suicide" ("Invisible," 39). This was the mood in which Mukherjee's second novel, *Wife* (1975), was written. Although she began the novel in Calcutta, and although most of the novel is set in New York and makes extensive use of that cityscape, *Wife* is shaded by the dark mood that had overtaken her in Canada. As Mukherjee explains her use of setting in the novel in "An Invisible Woman," "The nominal setting is Calcutta and New York City. But in the mind of the heroine [author?] it is always Toronto" ("Invisible," 39).

By the time "An Invisible Woman" was published in the Canadian magazine *Saturday Night* in March 1981, Mukherjee was in the United States as a permanent resident of that country. Living in New York, she was finding, was something of a relief. True, she had been robbed and attacked and cheated in the year or so she had already spent in the state, but at least she felt she was not being singled out for abusive treatment or being marginalized anymore or considered an outsider. In her opinion, American society at least allowed a new immigrant like her to slug it

out, while Canadian society degraded South Asians even though it per-
mitted them to be citizens.

In the first few years of her second period of residency in the United
States, Mukherjee continued to be rankled by her Canadian experience.
Indeed, the longer she stayed in America this time, the more she seemed
to remember her feeling of outrage in Canada and the more she began to
savor her stay in New York. Mukherjee's fourth book—*Darkness,* a
short-story collection published in 1984—reveals both her sense of frustration with Canada's policy of multiculturalism and her growing admi-
ration for America's melting-pot approach to immigration. At least
three of the stories of this collection are set in Canada and deal with the
threats and the tensions facing their South Asian characters as they
attempt to immerse themselves in that country; the rest of the stories are
set in the United States and are preoccupied with the problems South
Asian immigrants face in making contact and rooting themselves in
North America.

Mukherjee's polemical Preface to *Darkness* signals clearly her decision
to reject Canada, her commitment to the concept of expatriation she had
expressed earlier, and her eagerness to embark on a new phase of her life
in North America, where she would appear as the mytho-poet of immigration. As she explains in her Preface, until the spring of 1984, when
she wrote most of the stories collected in *Darkness* in a three-month period in Atlanta, Mukherjee had seen herself as an expatriate writer, someone who modeled herself on that ironic observer of immigrant fictional
worlds, the great West Indian writer V. S. Naipaul. Her Canadian fiction
was about immigrants who were basically "lost souls, put upon and
pathetic" (*Darkness,* 1), people she had fictionalized with "a state-of-the-
art expatriation" (*Darkness,* 2). That is to say, she had followed Naipaul's
practice of "using a mordant and self-protecting irony in describing" her
"characters' pain." A consequence is that the Canadian stories of the collection "are uneasy stories about expatriation," products of a mind that
was feeling "aggrieved" because it had weathered such hostility or indifference in the country.

Darkness, however, is a transitional work, and at least a few of the stories collected in this book are meant to capture something of the more
positive mood about migration to North America induced in Mukherjee
by her move to the United States in 1980. Gradually, she began to see
herself as just another immigrant and not a member of a "visible minority" as she was in Canada, targeted for abuse by an official policy of multiculturalism. Instead of holding on to her Indianness, Mukherjee could
now join "imaginative forces with an anonymous, driven underclass of

semi-assimilated Indians with sentimental attachments to a distant homeland but no real desire for permanent return." Bernard Malamud, a friend to whom *Darkness* is dedicated and for whom she had named one of her sons, now replaced Naipaul as her model, since what she would write about now was "the will to bond oneself to a new community, against the ever-present fear of failure and betrayal" (*Darkness*, 3).

Mukherjee wrote this "celebration" (*Darkness*, 4) of immigration to the United States in 1985 and became a full citizen of the country in 1988, but throughout the 1980s she continued to write about the predicament of South Asians in Canada. Thus, the second of the two books she co-authored with her husband, Clark Blaise, *The Sorrow and the Terror* (1987), and at least one of the stories collected in *The Middleman and Other Stories* (1988), "The Management of Grief," reflect her continuing preoccupation with Indians in Canada whose lives had been shattered by events—the origins of which she had no doubt could be traced to Canadian immigration policy. Both the collaborative work and the short story resulted from the investigation she and her husband carried on into the Air India plane crash of 1985. Their research confirmed Mukherjee in her belief that, looked at closely, Canada's vaunted multiculturalism was really a recipe for disaster.

In this chapter I focus on the fiction Mukherjee produced in the Canadian phase of her literary career and the work she continued to publish on Indian expatriates in Canada when in the United States. I also trace her moving away from this "dark" phase, although I argue that despite the upbeat note of the Introduction to *Darkness*, even the American stories of the collection are at least a little tinged with her doubts about the ability of Indian immigrants to succeed in assimilating themselves totally in American society. I consider in detail *Wife* and *Darkness* and look briefly at the argument of *The Sorrow and the Terror*. I do not, however, analyze "The Management of Grief," for even though the story centers on the impact of the Air India disaster on one woman's life, it moves away from the bitterness that dominates Mukherjee's fiction on expatriates in Canada and ends in hope in a way that makes it thematically a part of Mukherjee's work on immigrants in the United States.

Wife

Bharati Mukherjee's second novel has as its major theme the plight of an Indian wife torn between the need to play the role society expects of her and her need for self-expression. Another theme of the novel is her predicament as an Indian immigrant's wife in North America, since she can neither connect with the people around her nor give expression to her feeling of rage at her old life. Moreover, the novel tracks the violence building up inside and all around her in the North American landscape until she is driven to murder her husband.

Mukherjee has revealed in one of her published comments on the novel that the first of these themes—marriage as a pit for an Indian wife—suggested itself to her for fictional treatment when a visiting Columbia University professor asked her in Calcutta in 1974, "What do Bengali girls do between the age of eighteen and twenty-one?" (*Days*, 212). The sabbatical year she and Clark Blaise had spent in Calcutta made it appear to them that a young Bengali girl had very few options except to get married, and that if the marriage arranged for her by her parents did not work out, she had little else to look forward to. As Blaise explains it in his section of *Days and Nights in Calcutta,* the young girl "may end up—for she cannot refuse to marry—with a lout who will not tolerate the slightest deviation from expectancy, or the most pathetic gestures towards self-expression." And in Blaise's view *Wife* is "about such a girl . . . whose only available outlet, suicide, is transformed in the madness of emigration to New York into murder" (*Days,* 141). Or as Mukherjee phrases it in her portion of *Days and Nights in Calcutta, Wife* is about "a young Bengali wife who was sensitive enough to feel the pain, but not intelligent enough to make sense out of her situation and break out" (*Days,* 268). Mukherjee's anger at the predicament of Bengali wives in Calcutta merged with her own frustrations as an Indian immigrant in an intolerant Canada to give *Wife* the feel of a book bred in bitterness and tinged with violence. This is no doubt why Mukherjee has admitted in her 1990 *Iowa Review* interview that *Wife* "was a very painful book" for her to write (23).

But if a part of Mukherjee felt very close to Dimple Bose (née Dasgupta), it is important also to note that Mukherjee is quite distant from her heroine in other ways. Indeed, Mukherjee's choice of a limited third-person point of view is crucial to her overall strategy; this narrative perspective enables her "to stay close to Dimple—an immigrant wife who starts to question her traditional values—and show the immigrant world through her" (1987 interview, 36) while alerting us to her "inner inanities."[1] Dimple, in other words, is someone we are made to sympathize with, but someone whom we are also to view with irony because of her naïveté, instability, and even vacuity.

Dimple—the name is a popular one for girls in India, but as the epigraph of *Wife* reminds us, it suggests "a small surface depression"—is at the outset of this tripartite novel already showing at 20 the strains of waiting for a husband: "wasted years . . . lay like a chill weight in her body, giving her eyes a watchful squint and her spine a slight curve."[2] She even complains of chest pain and has to be hospitalized. In the hospital she dreams of Sita, "the ideal wife of Hindu legends, who had walked through fire at her husband's request" (*Wife*, 6), and fantasizes about sacrificing her own self for the sake of her husband. Reading *The Doctrine of Passive Resistance* for her examination, she can only imagine conquering her husband by her docility and coyness. Soon she is desperate enough to contemplate suicide as a way out of single life. Only marriage, she concludes, can save her and allow her to really live life.

But Dimple's marriage to Amit Kumar Basu, an engineer whose major qualification seems to be that he has applied for immigration to Canada and the United States, does not satisfy her for long. Living in a crowded apartment with her in-laws is, she discovers, as exacting as waiting for a husband. Now it is the strain of meeting other people's expectations that she finds unbearable. She discovers, for instance, that Amit had wanted her to be like Sita. She sees herself as a crow hurt by his slingshot, attempting to lift itself on its one good wing, only to fall down. She comes to dislike the idea of passive resistance and yearns for some dramatic gesture with which to impress Amit.

Gradually she begins to act in a manner that suggests that she would like to break out of the mold made for educated, middle-class Bengali wives like her if she only knew how. When she finds out that she is pregnant she thinks of getting rid of "whatever it was that blocked her tubes and pipes" (*Wife*, 31) and is filled with hatred against her husband and his parents. The rage welling up inside her finds a momentary outlet when she chases a mouse to the bathroom and smashes its head with a broom. It is as if by killing the mouse she was killing the part of herself that had been surviving by depending on others; what fascinates her about the dead creature is that it looked as pregnant as she was. Some time later she buys a goldfish only to flush it down the toilet in another attempt to purge the violence within her. Next, she scares cockroaches out of dark corners and then smashes them up. She envies her friend Pixie, who has definitely broken the mold by becoming an announcer for All-India Radio.

It is only after Amit comes home one day with the news that he has been accepted as an immigrant to the United States and after they start planning their move to North America that Dimple makes her first decisive attempt to rebel against the role fate seems to have reserved for her.

What she does then is literally skip her way into an abortion; since the baby would get in the way of the life full of possibilities that she thinks is awaiting her in North America, she had "picked a skipping rope as her weapon" (*Wife,* 43) against motherhood. As Maya Manju Sharma observes, unlike Tara Cartwright of *The Tiger's Daughter,* who "returns to India to recover her roots, Dimple Basu does everything she can to obliterate hers," inducing a miscarriage "so that she does not have to bring a child conceived in India into the New World," and adopting abortion as "a sacrament of liberation from the traditional roles and constraints of womanhood" (Sharma, 15).

And so Dimple arrives in New York in the second part of the novel, no longer having to worry about motherhood and full of hope because she will not have to carry on playing the role of the traditional Indian wife any more in this exciting new world. But she is a girl of limited intelligence, confined to the Indian immigrant community and the television set and cut off from a world that terrifies because it appears to be violent; once more she feels confused and traumatized by the turn of events. Although she thinks she is ready to venture forth in America, she is not really prepared for it and in no time gets depressed and starts to think of suicide and murder once more.

New York, and the life of Indian expatriates, at first seems appealing enough. Their Indian friends appear to be happy and prospering, and the bigness of the city strikes her as "thrilling" and only "a little scary" (*Wife,* 52). But there are disconcerting signs that she encounters but fails to read even on her first day in New York: talk of a triple murder that has just hit the radio waves indicates entry into a violent society, while a wall hanging of Sita "hip-deep in pale orange flames" (*Wife,* 53) in the apartment where they would be staying with Amit's friend Jyoti Sen and his family underscores her continuing membership in a community that puts a premium on a woman's ability to sacrifice herself for her family.

Life in America, however, at least allows Dimple to seek ways out of the role reserved for a wife in her community and to explore methods of breaking out of the mold made for the middle-class Indian woman. Significantly, she accepts as a friend and role model not Jyoti Sen's wife, Meena, who is content with motherhood and the comfortable life that immigration to America has brought her, but Ina Mullick, who is "more American than the Americans" (*Wife,* 68) in the sense that she is openly disdainful of her arranged marriage and is liberated and flirtatious. That Ina dresses skimpily and smokes and drinks in public and attends a night school fascinates Dimple, as does Ina's exhortation to her to get

out of the crisis of identity caused by entry into a new culture by thinking of herself as well as the white women around her as part of America.

It is quite obvious, then, that Dimple has come to America ready to
be transformed and willing to seek out an identity that would take her
away from the wifely ideals exemplified by Sita. And yet she fails to
break away from her South Asian community or connect with mainstream American society. Brinda Bose's comments in her perceptive
essay "A Question of Identity: Where Gender, Race, and America Meet
in Bharati Mukherjee" are very much to the point: "Dimple is helplessly
caught in the gripping quest for a new female American identity"; for
her, "a happy guiltless amalgamation seems impossible," and what goes
on inside her therefore is a "simultaneous fracturing and evolving of
identity."[3]

One major obstacle in Dimple's quest for identity is her husband.
Basically well-meaning but too absorbed initially in his search for economic security and later in adopting the mannerisms that will allow him
to survive in the marketplace, Amit does not have the time or the sensitivity to understand the complicated changes going on inside Dimple.
Although quite tolerant and considerate in some ways, he is too self-
absorbed and traditional to help his wife achieve selfhood. Husband and
wife, it is obvious, are traveling in opposite directions in North America,
and the gulf between them, just noticeable in Calcutta, opens up dramatically in New York. In Mukherjee's view, the process is a representative one:

> [When an Asian man comes to America] he comes for economic transfor-
> mation, and he brings a wife who winds up being psychologically
> changed. This is one of the tragedies you see being played out in all the
> New Jersey shopping malls these days. The Indian women walking
> around in the malls with nothing to do all day, while the men are out
> busily making money. The men have a sense of accomplishment. They
> have no idea of staying here. The idea is saving money and going. But
> they don't realize the women have been transformed. (1990 interview,
> 16)

Thus, although Amit is happy at one point that his wife is becoming
American, he is quite certain about one thing: he does not want her to
be "too American" (*Wife*, 112). He cannot think of letting her work,
even though she is bored and restless throughout the day and has nothing but her daydreams and the television set to occupy her then.

In her fantasies Dimple reconstructs Amit as a dashing hero of a newspaper advertisement or a television commercial. But even in the "Dewar's Profile" that she imagines for him, she has him cautioning her not to cross the limits imposed on Indian wives by convention and has him say, "Husbands should not permit wives to wear pants. A healthy society and mutual respect are based on the clear distinction between the appearance and the function of the sexes" (*Wife*, 158). When toward the end of the novel she almost freezes herself to death and Amit realizes for a moment that his wife is desperately unhappy, he can only diagnose her condition as the "culture shock" that all Indian wives in America go through, a condition to be distinguished from "one of those famous 'breakdowns' that American wives were fond of having" (*Wife*, 180). Little does he realize then or later that his wife is in fact disintegrating, and that a breakdown is something that an Indian woman can suffer from as much as American women.

Another obstacle in Dimple's path to self-realization is the expatriate Indian community in which she has to spend her time when with the Sens in the first few months of her stay in New York. As Janet M. Powers has concluded in an essay on Mukherjee's works, the parts of *Wife* dealing with the expatriate Indian community of New York amount to a "devastating critique of immigrant culture."[4] A woman such as Meena Sen is seen to be full of prejudice and quite parochial, suspicious of mixed marriages or of any Indian woman who dares to date someone from outside the expatriate community. She is also one of those women who become grief-stricken because they have another daughter instead of a male child. Her husband declares that if it was not for money, he would return to India. Husband and wife revel in America's consumer culture but have no desire to become part of the melting pot. They are typical of the Indian immigrants Dimple encounters in thinking of the United States as only a place to make a fortune and in dreaming of returning to India when they have amassed enough dollars for a comfortable retired life. Living in a kind of ghetto in Queens, they prefer to have the most superficial relationship with other Americans. Jyonti thus boasts that they never invite a white American over and asks, "Who needs *sahebs*? There must be a thousand Indians in just this neighborhood!" (*Wife*, 54). Men like Jyonti and Amit have a pervasive sense of insecurity about losing their jobs because of accusations of disorderly conduct and prefer not to risk anything at all by foraying into the world outside.

Inevitably, Dimple and her expatriate friends suffer from alienation in a culture whose codes they are not able to decipher. Even before Dimple had landed in New York, she had heard friends talk of America as a place where you could have fun but where you would have to be a foreigner all your life. At a farewell party given for her in Calcutta by Pixie, Dimple had been told by a woman who seemed to know all about South Asian expatriate life in North America, "*You* may think of it as immigration, my dear . . . but what you are is a *resident alien*" (*Wife*, 46). In New York, Dimple hears Meena confess how inadequate she feels outside her community because she has such a hard time understanding American humor or the English language. Dimple discovers in her first shopping expedition that it is difficult to do even the smallest chores in an alien culture when she asks for a cheesecake in a deli. Embarrassed by the response to her request, she finds herself then "caught in the crossfire of an American communalism she couldn't understand" (*Wife*, 60). At times Dimple thinks of talking to one of the American women she keeps meeting in the streets but decides that there are things she just could not ask them. Such thoughts inevitably lead to frustration and make her wonder how she could keep on living in a country "where every other woman was a stranger, where she felt different, ignorant, [and] exposed to ridicule in the elevator" (*Wife*, 112).

Nevertheless, Dimple keeps trying in her own confused and uncertain manner to put out feelers to see if she could immerse herself in this strange but exciting world. Moreover, she displays desires that indicate that she would like to break free from some of the habits of thought she had imbibed as a Bengali wife. She dreams of working and of going to night school, of throwing her own parties for friends, and of having her own flat where she could be herself. Not only does she feel attracted to Ina Mullick's unconventionality, but she is fascinated by Ina's white American sister-in-law, Marsha Mookerji, a university professor like her husband Prodosh Mookerji. She is visibly moved when Ina gives her a pamphlet advocating feminist ideas. Dimple's yearning to do something daring and to have new experiences can also be seen in the new ways in which she looks at men. Her husband appears to her to dwindle in importance in New York while she feels a stirring of sexual desire for Jyonti and for Marsha Mookerji's brother, Milt Glasser. In a conversation with Meena and Ina, Dimple implies that she sees nothing wrong in a marriage between a South Asian girl and an American male dancer; significantly, Meena finds the very idea disgusting. Yet at this stage of her

North American experience, Dimple knows that there are limits she should not transgress and is conscious that Amit would like her "to keep quiet and not make a fool of herself" (*Wife,* 89).

In the third part of *Wife* we get to see Dimple finally getting the opportunity to set up her own house after Amit lands a job and they decide to move for a while into a New York University apartment sublet to them for a term by Prodosh and Marsha Mookerji, who have taken sabbatical leave. But Dimple's anxieties and confusion about her identity increase when she finds herself alone for most of the day when Amit is out working. Her propensity for violence and tendency to take refuge in a fantasy world or slide into depression and irrational behavior are as evident in this section of the book as is her longing to acquire a new identity as an American woman. While she has more opportunities now for mixing with Americans and experimenting with an American life-style, she finds herself even more traumatized by the turn of events.

Why is Dimple's slide into madness precipitated precisely at the point when she has the opportunity to be all by herself and when she is free of the constraints imposed on an Indian wife by the constant presence of other members of her community? In her perceptive review of *Wife,* Linda Sandler suggests that Dimple goes crazy in part because of her own instability but mostly because she has moved into a social vacuum. In the Greenwich Village flat where she has to spend almost all her time watching television because she is too terrified of the violent world outside, her frustrations intensify, and she gets further unhinged from reality. As Sandler observes, *Wife* suggests that Dimple has moved into "a vacuum where once was society, and that violence becomes increasingly ordinary where there is no anchoring community."[5] In a short but incisive account of Bharati Mukherjee's work, Gita Rajan notes that *Wife* centers "on the debilitating, corrosive influence of an alien (and alienating) culture on a fragile self," and that Dimple's self is ultimately "shattered, detonated by a raw and alien reality."[6] It is pertinent to remember here, too, what Mukherjee herself has pointed out in "An Invisible Woman": *Wife* may be set in the American megalopolis, but metonymically she is writing about her own sense of insecurity in Toronto and her feeling of alienation in Canadian society.

The third part of *Wife* begins, therefore, with a Dimple who is desperately unhappy. She feels "like a star, collapsing inwardly" (*Wife,* 109) and is sure that something has gone dead inside her. She tells Amit that it is not homesickness that she is suffering from; what she does not tell him is that she no longer wants to act like Sita. She finds no one to talk to or share her thoughts with and takes to sleeping throughout the day. She had looked forward to an apartment of her own, but how could she have known that when all by herself her mind would be strained "beyond endurance," and how could she have anticipated such "inertia, exhaustion, endless indecisiveness" (*Wife,* 114)?

In her desperation, Dimple resumes her old habit of thinking of ways out of her predicament through suicide. She also contemplates attacking Amit, since he epitomizes those forces that seemed to trap and isolate her "in a high-rise full of Americans who ate hamburgers and pizzas" (*Wife,* 119). Of one thing she becomes certain: there was nothing to be gained by holding on to her memories of the past. On occasions, she is thrilled at the idea of living in a fully furnished apartment and the thought that she is in some way living Marsha's life by using her appliances and by wearing the white American woman's clothes. More positively, she begins to cultivate a relationship with Ina and, through her, with Milt Glasser. She is intrigued by the way Milt flirts with Ina and herself at parties and is aroused by the casual way he treats her and touches her.

But there are only so many parties that she can attend, and after every conversation with her few acquaintances she becomes even more depressed and conscious of being constricted in her New York apartment. Inevitably, she gets addicted to television, not realizing that the violence in her is further stimulated by it. The talk shows and soap operas she watches so compulsively corrode even more her already tenuous hold over reality. Her increasing inability to order her life is reflected in the disorder of her apartment. A bundle of nerves, she attacks Amit with a paring knife when he attempts to grab her from behind in sexual play; she is startled into thinking he is a rapist since "in America anything is possible. . . . You can be raped and killed on any floor" (*Wife,* 129), even the fourteenth. Although she is horrified by her own frenzy, she also begins to think that "perhaps she was capable of unimagined, calculating violence" (*Wife,* 130) and is even thrilled by Amit's vulnerability. Soon she alternates between self-pity and rage against Amit. Her only solace is the television set, and yet she does not realize that it is leading her to something terrible because "it was getting harder and harder to distinguish between what she had seen on TV and what she had imagined" (*Wife,* 157).

If, from one point of view, Dimple's neurosis signifies Mukherjee's frustration with the aloofness caused by expatriation, from another perspective the protagonist's mental turmoil represents the author's conviction that even such agonizing is a mark of progress. In her 1990 *Iowa Review* interview, Mukherjee declares that "in a bizarre way" her work "was meant to be optimistic," and that Dimple's arrival at a stage where she "learns to ask herself [such] 'self'-oriented questions [as] Am I happy? Am I unhappy?" is indicative of her progress towards self-realization (20). But since she has no clear idea about the goal she should be working toward or the means she should be using to assert herself effectively, these questions take her nowhere. Nevertheless, that there is an incipient feminist in Dimple is indicated by her approval of a conversation that takes place in her flat between Ina and her trendy feminist friend Leni Anspach "about being exploited by housework and afraid of self-expression and about avoiding confrontation" (*Wife,* 149). Dimple's next outburst, however, is directed at Leni, who has taken her dentures off to express her defiance of convention; as if to debunk such pretentious acts of self-assertion, Dimple pours tea all over Leni till she is forced to run out of the apartment with Ina. Dimple's bizarre behavior is meant to underline Mukherjee's contempt for fashionable feminists, even though it is quite clear that she has committed herself to writing sympathetically of the plight of Indian wives from a quasi-feminist perspective.

But Dimple's outbursts mark her as a manic-depressive for such spirited gestures or thoughts of rebellion from her are almost always followed by bouts of hopelessness. Although she thinks about "one extravagant gesture" she would like to make while still living (*Wife,* 153), her thoughts circle endlessly on death, dying, and dismemberment. She is conscious of being more and more alienated from her surroundings: "she was a pitiful immigrant among demanding appliances" (*Wife,* 186) in her New York University flat. She has premonitions of disaster. In one episode a strange man comes into her apartment, but it is difficult for the reader to ascertain whether he is really someone she encounters or a part of her fantasy life. When he leaves, she is certain of only one thing: nothing had happened between them. Still, "her imagination, inflamed by too many hours in front of the TV, pictured what might have been" (*Wife,* 161–62).

For a while it appears that Dimple's fantasies about a romantic stranger who will drop in and light up her life will come true through Milt Glasser. Even though he seems to be having an affair with Ina and is always accompanied by her, every encounter between him and Dimple brings them closer and closer to each other. Initially, she suffers from not knowing what his intentions are and whether he will kiss her or make love to her. It is obvious that he excites her and represents for her nothing less than the seductiveness of the New World; "he was, to her, America" (*Wife*, 174). With him, and with Marsha's clothes on her, she feels for the time being that "she could risk anything and get away with it" (*Wife*, 175). Milt seems to understand her and is ready to treat her as an individual and talk to her about all sorts of things. She is "amazed" that when out with him on one occasion, "the inhuman maze of New York became as safe and simple as Ballygunge" (*Wife*, 196), the district in Calcutta that she knew best.

When they return home from this outing they make love, and afterwards he promises to look after her and protect her from everything that seemed to be upsetting her. He seems to have understood her perfectly: "Everything about you is shocking and exciting and a little sad" (*Wife*, 201). And yet he is by his own admission only "halfway serious about things" (*Wife*, 199) and has other things to preoccupy him. And thus when he leaves her after this encounter she is as lonely and confused as ever, uncertain about his intentions and even more cut off than before from her husband and her community. She has traveled as far as she could in her quest to gain a new identity and yet is no closer to her goal of achieving self-fulfillment in America. Her desire to unite with an American has taken her to a dead end, while she has experienced enough of expatriate life to know that she cannot stand it anymore.

Given the trajectory of Dimple's progress in America, the conclusion of *Wife* is inevitable: she must resort to some violent and extreme action to get out of the bind that expatriation to America has gotten her into. Still, her way to resolve her dilemma is shocking: just as she had seen happen on television shows many a time, she sneaks up behind Amit and then stabs him to death. After all, had she not seen enough on the screen to realize that "women on television got away with murder" (*Wife*, 213)?

Mukherjee has gone on record to state that even though the ending of the novel is "discomfiting," she wanted readers to treat Dimple's decision to murder her husband as "a misguided act of self-assertion" and as evidence of her "slow and misguided Americanization" (1987 interview, 44) and of progress of sorts for a woman otherwise fated to obliterate herself or end her life. Dimple, in Mukherjee's view, had just killed the enemy, the major obstacle in her progress toward selfhood and immersion in the brave new world of America, and she had done so by "utilizing the tools at hand" (1990 interview, 16). The anger that Mukherjee had felt at the plight of Bengali wives in Calcutta during her sabbatical year in the city had combined with her bitterness at being denied admission into mainstream Canadian society to make *Wife* a "wounding novel" (*Days,* 268).

In any event, *Wife* did manage to rattle a number of its readers. Some feminists felt that the book recommended passivity as a means of resistance, while in her review of the book in *Ms.* Rosanne Klass was scathing about its message that knifing a husband was a way out of the Indian immigrant woman's problems in New York.[7] Many Indian critics were repelled by Mukherjee's premise that most Indian wives are doomed to living desperate lives. One Indian critic, Jasber Jain, found fault with *Wife* both from the feminist and Indian points of view; according to Jain, Dimple is too abnormal and involved in a dream world to be portrayed as either a victim of patriarchal society or of expatriation. Jain implies that Mukherjee is wrong to attribute all of Dimple's problems to the limitations placed on Indian wives or on the state of alienation induced in her by the move to New York, since "she is unable to find or realize herself in any context for her value system has never been structured."[8] Certainly it would appear that Mukherjee vitiates her critique of the forces that have contributed to Dimple's crack-up by making her inherently unstable and by giving her an ingrained tendency to veer away from reality. As Martin Levin observed in his *New York Times Book Review,* "However oppressed Dimple may be, she is also very crazy, a fact about which the author is amusing but ambiguous. You could raise Dimple's consciousness by ninety degrees and still have a zombie."[9]

Nevertheless, *Wife* also received many favorable reviews when it was published and has been widely praised for its portrayal of Indian expatriates in North America and its depiction of one immigrant woman's twisted progress toward acquiring a new self on the continent. Mukherjee has also been admired for her insight into the effects of media violence on fragile individuals. In her essay on Bharati Mukherjee in *International Literature in English: Essays on the Modern Writers,* Liew-Geok Leong thus admires the novel for taking "the psychology and geography of displacement as far as possible in its terse pursuit of disaster."[10] Mukherjee's book has also been praised for its skillful use of its Calcutta and New York settings and for almost surreal scenes that convey Dimple's descent into madness in her New York flat. As in *The Tiger's Daughter*, Mukherjee's adept use of a narrative tone that combines irony and sympathy was appreciated. No one has mentioned, however, her skills in parodying advice columns, magazine advertisements, talk-show inanities, and other popular discourses, or her skills in reproducing the way Indians in America speak or in capturing Americanisms.

Technically, *Wife* represents an advance in Mukherjee's art over her first novel in being less consciously literary and more original. It is difficult thus to track down influences on this book unlike on *The Tiger's Daughter,* since Mukherjee pares down the number of allusions to other literary works, although she herself has acknowledged the influence of Naipaul in her ironic portrayal of expatriate life-styles. Dimple's letters to "Miss Problem-walla"—an Indian newspaper's version of Ann Landers—may have as their source situations in Nathanael West's *Miss Lonelyhearts.* Maya Manju Sharma has made the interesting observation that the way Mukherjee manages to evoke out of apparently frivolous situations "deep and sinister" notes indicate that Flannery O'Connor "is a clear influence" (Sharma, 15). Also, the many grotesque elements of the novel and its violent ending evokes O'Connor and affiliates it with the contemporary American Gothic. If this is really the case, and if Mukherjee has taken inspiration in this novel from writers such as West and O'Connor, that in itself marks a significant step in her movement away from being a writer preoccupied with exile or the British tradition of Jane Austen and E. M. Forster to a writer placing herself consciously in a North American tradition of immigrant writing.

Darkness

In the interview she gave to Geoff Hancock a couple of years after the publication of *Darkness,* Bharati Mukherjee attributes the writing of the volume to two factors: her move from Canada to the United States in 1980 and her reading of Bernard Malamud's *Selected Stories* (1983). Apparently her growing frustration at Canada's policy of multiculturalism, her firsthand experience of racism in Toronto and Montreal, and her indignation at being passed over by Canada's literary establishment despite the largely favorable reviews received by her first two novels and *Days and Nights in Calcutta* constricted Mukherjee for a period and prevented her from coming up with something that would further consolidate her reputation as a writer in Naipaul's tradition. As she explains it to Hancock, moving out of Canada gave back her voice after seven years during which she was forced to see herself "as part of an unwanted 'visible minority'" (1987 interview, 42). It was almost as if the stories collected in *Darkness* emerged as soon as she could free herself "from the feelings of anger and powerlessness brought on by the racism" she experienced in Canada (1987 interview, 33). As for the effect Malamud had on her, she notes that although she and her husband had known the celebrated Jewish-American novelist for over 20 years, it was reading his *Selected Stories* in her second extended trip to the United States that made her want to write *Darkness*. She feels strongly that Malamud "brought out the best" in the couple's fictions, and that his "compassion and wisdom" was an ideal she could attempt to emulate (1987 interview, 40).

In another interview given to Alison B. Carb, Mukherjee explains in greater detail why she chose Malamud as a model at a time in her career when she wanted to move away from stories of frustrated expatriates in Canada to narratives that celebrated the resilience of the new wave of South Asian immigrants in the United States in the 1980s. To her, Malamud and not Naipaul could help her set the agenda for her fiction now, since he wrote so well "about a minority community which escapes the ghetto and adapts itself to the dominant American culture," and since his work "seems to find quite naturally a moral center" (1988 interview, 650). Mukherjee, of course, is aware that her fiction was bound to be different from Malamud's because of her gender, skin color, and religious beliefs, but she has no doubt that she was now placing herself in a literary tradition where he had to be acknowledged as a literary ancestor.

Taking her cue from the interview Mukherjee gave to Carb, Carol Stone has further traced the nature of Mukherjee's indebtedness to Malamud. To Stone, what affiliates the Indian writer to the Jewish-American one is that both "write about immigrant experience in America, about the struggle to overcome being viewed as 'the Other.'"[11] True, Malamud focuses almost entirely on the male immigrant character as a *schlemiel,* while Mukherjee increasingly upholds for us "the female immigrant as a conquering heroine," but what is of greater interest is the way their fictions deal with "the diasporic experience of cultural alienation" and "the remaking of oneself as an American" (Stone, 214).

It is important for us to realize, however, that only a few of the 12 stories collected in *Darkness* were written out of Mukherjee's sense of relief at the move that had brought her away from Canada and had made her a landed immigrant in the United States. Similarly, it is noteworthy that Mukherjee is not able to replace Naipaul completely with Malamud as her diasporic literary model in these stories. Indeed, the polemical Introduction to *Darkness* shows clear signs of being written after the stories themselves; its upbeat tone and aggressive celebration of "the exuberance of immigration" will mislead only a few readers of the volume into believing that her overwhelming concern is not still for characters who suffer from "the aloofness of expatriation" and who would like to embrace America but fail to do so because of some lack in them or in the world around them (*Darkness,* 3).

The best way to approach *Darkness,* then, is to see it as a collection of stories that reveals a variety of responses to immigration to North America. In other words, while a few of the stories show immigrants striving to root themselves in North America, most approach the plight of expatriates on the continent soberly and even with a touch of despair. If Malamud's humanism has inspired some of Mukherjee's tales of immigrant lives, others employ the kind of irony she had learned from Naipaul in presenting people who cannot or will not graft themselves into another culture. Also, it is important to keep in mind that by calling the collection *Darkness,* Mukherjee is deliberately reminding us of Conrad's grim novella about human nature as revealed in extreme situations of cultural displacement.

In fact, what is remarkable about the book is Mukherjee's conscious attempt to embrace the experience of all kinds of immigrants to Canada and the United States. According to Mukherjee, it was as the writer-in-residence at Emory University in the winter 1984 semester that she found herself suddenly bursting with narratives of immigrant experiences. Drawing on her own memories as well as the experiences of her South Asian friends and acquaintances, and relying in some cases on newspaper reports, she began to produce story after story about the lot of the Indian immigrant in America. As she explains it in the essay "A Four-Hundred-Year-Old Woman," she began to see herself and her "own experience refracted through a dozen separate lives" ("Woman," 25). A direct consequence of this burst of creativity and receptivity to South Asian immigrant lives is the wide range of characters assembled in *Darkness*: illegal and legal immigrants, first- and second-generation North Americans, rich and poor South Asians on the continent, professionals as well as migrant or menial workers, all now appeal to the storyteller in Mukherjee.

Corresponding to this great variety of characters, Mukherjee experiments in the volume with a number of perspectives and settings. Thus "Angela," the first story, is written from the point of view of a Bangladeshi girl who has been adopted by a family in Iowa after she had been orphaned by Pakistani soldiers attempting to suppress her people's struggle for independence. "The Lady from Lucknow," the second story, also uses the first-person point of view, although the narrator now is a middle-aged Muslim woman called Nafeesa Hafeez who has settled in Atlanta with her husband after a life full of diasporic moves across several continents. The next story, "The World According to Hsü," returns to the omniscient mode of storytelling Mukherjee used in her first two novels. But as in those works, Mukherjee's omniscient narrator presents the story mostly from the point of view of a married woman. In this case, she is Ratna Clayton, a 33-year-old Canadian journalist of mixed origins vacationing in an island off the coast of the southernmost part of Africa, which may or may not be Madagascar.

"A Father," the fourth story of *Darkness,* also uses an omniscient narrator reflecting events from the perspective of the protagonist, a middle-aged expatriate engineer from Bihar, India, who has made Detroit his home. This tale is followed by "Isolated Incidents," the only story in the book where an omniscient narrator focuses on a white Canadian woman called Ann Vane who works in a Human Rights Office in Toronto. Mukherjee employs the omniscient mode also for the sixth story, "Nostalgia." This tale, set in New York City, follows the middle-aged psychiatric consultant Dr. Manny Patel as he tries to enjoy a tryst with an attractive Indian salesgirl in a Manhattan hotel. Mukherjee reverts to the first-person mode in "Tamurlane" although all we know about the narrator is that he is one of a number of illegal Indian immigrants from the Indian province of Punjab who works in a hotel in Toronto. Leela Lahiri, a Bengali Brahmin woman employed as an administrative assistant in a New York publishing firm, narrates the subsequent story, titled "Hindus."

"Saints," the ninth story of *Darkness,* is another first-person narrative. Its narrator, Shawn Patel, is the son of Dr. Manny Patel of "Nostalgia"; now, however, the setting is a small college town in upstate New York where Shawn and his mother have moved after his parents separated. In "Visitors" Mukherjee returns to omniscient storytelling. She puts her protagonist in a New Jersey setting and a situation somewhat like that of *Wife.* The penultimate story of *Darkness,* "The Imaginary Assassin," really employs two narrators, for in it a young Sikh boy growing up in Yuba City, California, records a story his grandfather tells him about the circumstances that led him to flee India in 1947. Only the concluding story is not about the experience of immigration to North America. Indeed, "Courtly Vision," is not a story in any conventional sense of the term but a description of a Mughal painting that Mukherjee uses as a metaphor for the miniaturist's vision of immigrant lives that she has drawn for us in her collection of tales.

Despite the wide variety of immigrant character types assembled in *Darkness* and the diverse narrative modes put to use in the stories, it is possible to divide them into groups on the basis of their subject matter and tone. "The World According to Hsü," "Isolated Incidents," and "Tamurlane" are the "Canadian" stories of the collection. Not by coincidence, they are also stories of the "aloofness of expatriation"—bitter tales of people who cannot root themselves in Canadian culture because of covert or overt racism in the country. Although set in the United States, "A Father" and "Nostalgia" deal with South Asian men who cannot stop seeing themselves as expatriates and who still yearn for some of the values or images associated with the country of their birth. While "Saints" and "The Imaginary Assassin" contrast sharply in subject matter and focus, they can be grouped together because they both have as their narrators immigrant youths born in North America who are attracted to Indian stories about saintly figures. "The Lady from Lucknow" and "Visitors" resemble each other in that they are about Indian wives who are frustrated in their attempt to find fulfillment outside their marriages. Only "Angela" and "Hindus" can be considered as stories written about characters who have successfully liberated themselves from the country where they were born to accept America, but even in these narratives Mukherjee emphasizes that you cannot eradicate your past and hope for total acceptance in the New World. And as I have already indicated, "Courtly Vision" is sui generis and really should not be viewed as a story at all.

Perhaps the best story of the collection, "The World According to Hsü," is a clear proof that despite what Mukherjee has herself said in her Introduction, she has not been able to shake off Naipaul as an influence. As Anita Desai, one of India's leading novelists, has commented in a shrewd review of the volume in *London Magazine,* the story "could have been written by him, this tale of an estranged couple's visit to an island off the coast of Africa suddenly struck by a coup and curfew; it has the same grey melancholy, the same way of picking out the telling detail "that has become Naipaul's trademark."[12] For the wife, Ratna Clayton, the vacation she and her academic husband, Graeme, are taking brings to the surface all the tension bottled up in her. Graeme has insisted on the vacation because he had hopes that it "would be the right setting for persuading Ratna to move to Toronto, where he had been offered . . . the chair in Personality Development" (*Darkness,* 40–41). But although Graeme is already a full professor of psychology at McGill, he is quite obtuse and cannot understand that she does not want to settle in Toronto because there she was "not Canadian, not even Indian. She was something called, after the imported idiom of London [racism], a Paki. And for Pakis, Toronto was hell" (*Darkness,* 41). Despite her origins (her mother was Czech and her father Bengali), her sense of her identity (she considers herself to be completely Canadian), and her affinity for things European, Ratna is destined to be abused as a "Paki."

Ratna knows that in some things she would always be typecast because of the color of her skin. Even the taxi driver who had been taking her and Graeme around the island takes it for granted that she is an Indian married to a white American. Because the coup has led to riots where mobs have attacked grocery stores run by South Asians, Ratna should feel threatened in the island. Surprisingly, however, she feels quite safe there; all her fears are about Toronto and what could happen to her there. Graeme, quite insensitive to her thoughts on moving, assures her that nothing will happen to her in the Canadian city, but what flashes through her mind while he talks are newspaper reports of South Asians brutalized on the streets of Toronto by racists. And so, while "jeering paratroopers who pointed their rifles and fired mock salvos into their taxi," drive past them, she feels "safer than she had in the subway stations of Toronto" (*Darkness,* 49). At their hotel dinner table Graeme reads to her from a *Scientific American* piece by someone called Kenneth J. Hsü about continents shifting, but her thoughts slide from the article to Graeme's plans to move and she ends up feeling that she had become "an expert on the plate techtonics of emotion" (*Darkness,* 55). Later, while they are sipping wine, they hear that the situation on the island has deteriorated even further. Soon afterwards, Graeme reveals to her that the move to Toronto was really a fait accompli, for he had already accepted the post offered to him by the University of Toronto. As the tale comes to an end, Graeme leaves to view the Southern Cross, and Ratna finds herself in a roomful of refugees babbling in different languages. She should be feeling miserable and afraid in this environment, given the violence outside the hotel and the tumult within her, but paradoxically, she is certain that "no matter where she lived, she would never feel so at home again" (*Darkness,* 56).

The ending of "The World According to Hsü" is thus an implicit indictment of people like Graeme, who embody the Canadian liberal establishment's insensitivity and complacence about racism in the country. It is a bitter tale written from the perspective of a woman who has concluded that Canada will never allow her to root herself in it and who is convinced that she was destined to be an eternal expatriate. A similar perspective controls the telling of "Isolated Incidents," a story that traces a fairly routine day in the life of a white Canadian social worker named Ann Vane. This story shows Ann working in her Human Rights Office where she has to deal with one complaint after another from immigrants from morning till noon. On this day, for instance, she has to go through the file dealing with the case of Dr. Supariwala, a woman from Bombay who has complained about discrimination in the workplace. Apparently, Dr. Supariwala has been consistently passed up in job interviews in Canada, despite her clearly superior qualifications and track record of dedicated service because of "certain half-articulated, coded objections" that have nothing to do with her ability and everything to do with her origins *(Darkness,* 79). And yet what amazes Ann is that every day she has to deal with "the Supariwalas [who] wanted to stay on."

Another case she has to work through on this day is that of a Mr. Hernandez, who has decided to contact the Human Rights Office because he thinks that Immigration Canada is unfairly preventing him from sponsoring his sister's stay in the country after the visitor's visa issued to her under her estranged husband's name expires. A third case she has to tackle on that day involves a John Mohan Persawd, an immigrant from Guyana who had been assaulted in a Toronto subway by a racist gang. Working through such cases, Ann habitually puts on "her practised look of demure commiseration" *(Darkness,* 78) even though it is quite clear that her capacity to feel for her clients has diminished. After all, the police always treated the complaints she had to investigate as "isolated incidents," and preferred not to label them as "racial in nature" *(Darkness,* 83), while she herself had to handle them day after day and had come to accept that nothing could be or would be done about them. And yet, when the aggrieved Guyanan declares bitterly, "Canadians are mean as hell. . . . Life is hopeless, man, no justice, no redress" *(Darkness,* 84), Ann cannot help defending her country by offering a specious argument: "I don't know about that. . . . If this had happened in New York, you'd have been left for dead."

As far as Mukherjee seems to be concerned, however, the true distinction between violence in Toronto and violence in New York is that made by Prasad's lawyer, who corrects Ann by saying, "If this had happened in New York, he'd have been mugged for his money, not racially assaulted." In other words, racism was becoming endemic in Canada whereas crime in New York had only socioeconomic causes. The lawyer also seems to be Mukherjee's mouthpiece in pointing out that people like Ann were taking the easy way out by disclaiming any responsibility for such acts of violence. It seems to be Mukherjee's contention that liberal Canadians tend to deny the fact of ever-present racism; it is as if ignoring the problem will make it go away.

If "Isolated Incidents" had ended at this point it could have been easily dismissed as only a thinly veiled polemic against racism in Canadian society. But what complicates the narrative is the manner in which Mukherjee uses the one meeting in Ann's day that has nothing to do with her work to make a deeper point about Canadian society. While going through the three cases during the morning, Ann keeps constantly thinking about her lunchtime appointment with her school friend Poppy, now famous as Peppi Paluka, the lead vocal of a Los Angeles band. Unlike Ann, who had moved from Montreal to Toronto and had downgraded her expectations from life by accepting the security of a bureaucratic job, Poppy had opted for flamboyance and had ended up a celebrity. Ann's life was one of compromises, of roads not taken. For example, she had once shown promise as a poet but could not write anymore. Talking, therefore, to her now-famous friend, Ann keeps seeing her life as a diminished thing. There is a "dour reasonableness" about Canada that she had inevitably imbibed and that had inhibited her emotionally (*Darkness*, 87). By contrast, Ann realizes, even the immigrants she had to encounter every day were bold and enterprising people who had hazarded their all to make a life for themselves in a new world. And even though "not everyone had done well . . . they had taken a chance" (*Darkness*, 87). Not surprisingly, therefore, Ann, and Canadians like her, are haunted by failure while the immigrants seem to have the capacity for growth and a desire to fight adversity that hinted at eventual success.

Mukherjee, then, manages to evoke a certain amount of compassion for Ann and the pain in her soul. But while allowing some sympathy for the individual, Mukherjee has no intentions of letting Canadian government policy off the hook. "Isolated Incidents" thus ends with a confrontation between Ann and Mr. Hernandez at a Kentucky Fried Chicken franchise where she has stopped on her way back from her meeting with Poppy to have lunch. When he sees her in the fast-food place, Mr. Hernandez immediately grabs the opportunity to remind her that something should be done to let his sister stay in Canada. But Ann reverts to her usual response when faced with such importunateness: she tightens up inside and reminds Mr. Hernandez of the inflexibility of

Canadian immigration laws. Soon, the frustrated man begins shouting at her and petitioning her with seemingly aggressive gestures. As with the ending of "The World According to Hsü," there is an indictment of liberal Canada in his impassioned outcry, "You people cannot feel, that is the problem" (*Darkness*, 92). Unlike the earlier story of the collection, however, Mukherjee ends this one by making us commiserate at least a little with Ann, who is shown at the end to be a pathetic figure, overwhelmed with self-pity because of Mr. Hernandez's outburst, and unable to cope with him because of the smallness of her own life and the rigidity of her country's laws.

In "Tamurlane," however, Mukherjee has no intentions of sparing anybody, and her indictment of Canadian society in this tale is savage and total. At the heart of the story is a brutal confrontation between Canadian mounties and immigration officers who are raiding a Toronto Indian restaurant because they have information that it is run mostly by illegal workers from South Asia. Gupta, its chef, is a man who has not lost faith in Canada despite being crippled when he was pushed in front of a Toronto subway train by a racist gang. He has an offer to work in a new restaurant in the United States from a recruiting agent, but he prefers to stay on, prizing the citizenship he has won over the promise of a better salary. He seems not to be deterred by his past experience or by the comments of his owner that "Canadians don't want Asian immigrants" (*Darkness*, 118) or the story he hears of a Dr. Chowdhury who left his $70,000 practice because he had had enough of racial discrimination.

Although "Tamurlane" comes to a climax in the fatal encounter between the agents of the law and Gupta, Mukherjee decides to present the story from the perspective of an illegal immigrant to explain why Gupta values his Canadian citizenship regardless of the dangers he faces in staying on in a country hostile to South Asian immigrants. The anonymous narrator is one of three illegal immigrants who work in the restaurant. They have to sleep on the floor and are constantly harried by the police, but they have already invested a fortune to come to Canada to work and must earn enough to recoup their investment. To people like them, the difference between a legal immigrant and an illegal one is immense. Gupta knows that there are thousands of illegal immigrants spread across North America who would like to get legal status. Having somehow become a legal immigrant, Gupta is not willing to trade his citizenship for anything else, even though a recruiting agent cautions him, "If you stay here, trouble's going to find you" (*Darkness*, 120).

And trouble does find Gupta in the combined mounties-immigration raid on the restaurant. A mountie and an immigration officer collar the illegal immigrants and order Gupta to come along with them. Indignant, Gupta asserts his right to be in the restaurant and asks the officials to leave. In the heated exchange that follows, the mountie attempts to grab Gupta while the chef retaliates by attacking the mountie with a cleaver. The mountie is badly injured but manages to shoot Gupta, who is able only to flash his passport in front of his face as if to establish his claim to be in Canada despite all the hate, suspicion, and bodily blows directed at his kind in the country. It is a scene that makes for a bloody climax to a very angry story. Patricia Bradbury is surely right when she observes that the "swift but violent struggle" at the end amounts to "a ruthless and tragic mockery" of Gupta's decision to remain in Canada.[13]

If Canada represents a dead end for the likes of Gupta, and his faith in the country is seen to be tragically misplaced at the end of the story, immigration to the United States appears as an attractive option for some of the other characters in the story. Indeed, Mukherjee suggests throughout "Tamurlane" that most South Asian immigrants in Canada were already turning their eyes south of the border and that Indians were beginning to settle throughout the United States. The owner of the Toronto restaurant where the action of the story takes place is thus said to have opened a 67-unit motel in Florida. The firm of Khanna & Sons of Buffalo, New York, is described as specializing in the manufacture of the type of oven required in Indian cooking, presumably because there is a big market for this product now in the United States. Mohan, the busboy of the restaurant, wants to go to New York or Miami, since he knows that thousands of South Asians were flocking there every day. The recruiting agent in the restaurant who tries to lure Gupta away to America talks about cities such as Dallas, Atlanta, or Fort Worth, which are "safe" for Indian immigrants. Apparently, the opening of new Indian restaurants has made men with his skills in demand in America's big cities and such restaurants have opened even in the middle of Harlem. It is as if Mukherjee, always very careful about every detail in her fiction, is alerting her readers to the demographic transformations that were taking place in America in the 1970s and the 1980s as a wave of legal and illegal immigrants from South Asia spread throughout the country.

In "An Invisible Woman," written a year after she left Canada to settle in the United States for a second time, and three years before she wrote most of the stories of *Darkness,* Mukherjee describes the difference between the country she had left in 1966 and the country to which she had returned in 1980. In 1966 a South Asian like her "was an exotic in America, except in university towns and maybe New York City," whereas now she doubted if "there's a town in America without its Indian family—even Saratoga Springs [where she had settled in 1980] has Indian dentists and pediatricians" ("Invisible," 39). No longer an exotic, and not, according to Mukherjee, a target of racial abuse as in Canada, these Indians had become interesting subjects for a storyteller like her. Not all of them were succeeding in rooting themselves in the United States, of course, and many of them had already botched up their lives by failing to adapt to a new world, but that only made them more fascinating to her.

Mr. Bhowmick, the protagonist of "A Father," for example, is the type of man who intrigues Mukherjee because he is obsessed with the thought of failure despite all his trappings of worldly success. As a metallurgist working in Detroit, and with a wife who is employed as a claims investigator in an insurance company and a daughter who is an electrical engineer, Mr. Bhowmick should be enjoying life and reveling in his ownership of expensive items such as the Rolex watch he looks at when he gets up every morning. Certainly, the women in his household have no problems in facing life, but then they "were cheerful, outgoing, more American somehow" (*Darkness,* 61). He, on the other hand, has premonitions of disaster, cannot quite connect with his Americanized daughter, Babli, or even his white American neighbor, and keeps holding on to the beliefs and practices of his native land. Nevertheless, he has no intention of going back to the country he had left.

Mr. Bhowmick's problem, then, is that he can neither let go of the past nor embrace the present. When he discovers quite by chance that Babli is pregnant, his ambivalence about his life in America is on display again. At first he is upset, and all his suspicions and insecurities grip him. Then he gets a little excited by the thought that his daughter, whom he had always considered as unfeminine by his (Indian male) standards of femininity, had at least been loved by some man. Then he is tormented by the thought of the shame brought on his family by an illegitimate grandchild. Was he to praise or curse the expatriate life that had brought him such a surprise? Looking around for a scapegoat, he finds one in his wife, who had driven him to migrate to the United States. But he knows in his soul that he had not liked the life they had led or the job he did in India and had wanted out of his native country as much as she did. Eventually, Mr. Bhowmick comes to realize that he would have to accept Babli's lover as well as the child, although "an American son-in-law was a terrifying notion" (*Darkness,* 71). When in the surprising climax of "A Father," however, Mr. Bhowmick suddenly finds out that his daughter had decided to become pregnant through a sperm bank since she wanted a baby but not a father, he goes berserk and attacks her with a rolling pin.

Commenting on the bizarre and violent ending of the story, Mitali R. Pati declares that "Mr. Bhowmick's violence symbolizes patriarchy gone mad in its own powerlessness" and reminds us of a tale remembered by the protagonist of "The Lady from Lucknow." In that tale a Muslim girl dies of a broken heart after her Muslim father beats her up for falling in love with a Hindu boy.[14] While Pati may be right in saying that Mr. Bhowmick becomes insane because he feels that his daughter has some- how taken away what he thinks of as his right to choose a man for her, it is important to realize that the main reason that Mr. Bhowmick loses his control is that his daughter's radical decision has made it impossible for him to conceal the discrepancy between his orthodox Indian beliefs and his American life-style anymore. We need to note also that the ending of "A Father" resembles closely the conclusion of Mukherjee's second novel, *Wife,* for Mr. Bhowmick's attack on his daughter is as desperate and as grotesque an act as Dimple's destruction of Amit, even though Mukherjee treats the father of the story with considerable cynicism while the heroine of the novel draws mostly her sympathy.

Throughout "A Father" Mukherjee shows us Mr. Bhowmick contin- ually looking back at the past since he cannot give up the values or standards he had acquired from his native land. Dr. Manny Patel of "Nostalgia," the sixth story of *Darkness,* also yearns for some of the icons of his youth, as if there is a lack in the life that he is leading as a psychiatric resident at a state hospital in Queens, New York. Dr. Patel's recurring desire is for an affair with an Indian girl, and the romantic in him seems to think that he needs to go outside his marriage with his white American wife, Camille, to find true sexual fulfillment. Thus, he is attracted by a nubile Indian salesgirl, Padma, whom he sees while passing the store she works in in New York City's bustling "Little India" district. Padma—the name for a beautiful tropical lotus associ- ated with Lakshmi, the Hindu goddess of love and beauty—appears to him to personify the feminine ideals perpetuated in popular Indian films and romantic poetry. That she responds to his overtures instantly only serves to convince him that all his erotic fantasies are about to come true.

Dr. Patel is not thoroughly dissatisfied with the life he is leading in America. On the contrary, he is grateful to be working in New York, where he has so many patients that he can afford to lead a life of luxury. In fact, Dr. Patel is enthusiastic about America and loves his showy house and his red Porsche, despite having to suffer patients such as the schizophrenic Mr. Horowitz who, in one outburst, had called him "Paki scum." He even has some affection for Camille and positively loves their son, Shawn, whom he has placed at Andover. He knows that he has saved enough money to go back to India as a millionaire, but he is only too conscious about how well he is doing in America.

Nevertheless, although "America had been very good to him . . . there were things that he had given up" (*Darkness,* 99)—for instance, people like his parents whom he missed very much, and Indian food and traditions. Caught in a bind like Mr. Bhowmick's, "he knew he would forever shuttle between the old world and the new" and was aware that "he couldn't pretend he had been reborn when he became an American citizen" (*Darkness,* 105). This is the reason that when he sees Padma in the Indian shop in a T-shirt and navy corduroys, he has an overwhelming desire to dress her in a sari and worship and possess her. And when she responds with alacrity to his diffident advances and proposes a date, he is thrilled. He silences all his scruples about adulterous conduct, "as though if he let up for a minute, his reconstituted, instant American life would not let him back" (*Darkness,* 103). Wandering through the shops and restaurants of "Little India" where "the Manhattan air . . . was fragrant with spices," he has the heady feeling that he was about to play a leading part in a romance. Taking the girl to a hotel room, he is almost triumphant because he has the feeling that in his daring he had finally "laid claims to America" (*Darkness,* 110).

As in "A Father," however, Mukherjee is writing in a satiric vein here and, if anything, she is parodying the romance mode in this tale. No wonder, then, that in the dénouement of "Nostalgia" all of Dr. Patel's illusions about romance are shattered in the hotel room just after he has made love to Padma when she reveals herself to be a prostitute employed by a blackmailer who not only demands money from Dr. Patel but also a letter from him so that he can convince the immigration office to let the girl stay in America. Disabused of his regressive fantasies, Dr. Patel is shown at the grotesque and somewhat forced conclusion of the tale to be painting "whore" on the mirror of the hotel room with his excrement in an act of revenge as well as a gesture suggesting his renunciation of his Indian romantic fantasies.

Ruing his decision to woo Padma near the end of "Nostalgia," Dr. Patel understands that one reason he had fallen for her so readily is that while she had appeared to him to be like an Indian goddess, she had also attracted him by displaying what he considers the liberated American woman's insouciance about sex. Or, as the narrator puts it, "He had mistaken her independence as a bold sign of honest assimilation" (*Darkness*, 112). What he realizes now is that "it was his son [Shawn Patel] who was the traveller over shifting sands, not her." "Saints," the ninth story of *Darkness*, is about this son and his perilous progress in a brave new world. In this story Dr. Patel and Camille have separated, and their son, Shawn, is living with his mother, who has got a job in an upstate New York college. His parents' break-up has made him sensitive, and he claims that "at fifteen I'm too old to be a pawn between them, and too young to get caught in problems of my own," and is really "in a state of grace" (*Darkness*, 146). But while he can be extraordinarily clear-eyed about some things, he is also, Mukherjee implies, afflicted by alienation and at times close to hysteria. It is not surprising, then, that he finds solace only in the company of other multiracial youths and that he has a secret life of his own.

Shawn Patel, in fact, is a very complex character, and "Saints" is one of the most ambivalent and best stories of *Darkness*. In his long and helpful *Canadian Literature* review of the volume, Peter Nazareth observes that the story resembles the "saint" stories of J. D. Salinger but that because Mukherjee's protagonist, unlike Salinger's adolescents, has "a more complex inheritance," his "search is not to preserve innocence but to find wholeness."[15] Shawn inhabits a fragmented world, is cut off from his South Asian father (whom, in any case, he does not understand), and is estranged from his mother, who is, he knows, being cheated on by her lover. He treads through an America peopled by insensitive authority figures—like his schoolteacher, who makes his best friend, Tran, narrate his experience as a Vietnamese boat person—and by middle-class immigrants from South Asia and Central and Eastern Europe. He must carve out his own sense of identity in this fluid, constantly changing landscape.

One possible place where Shawn can get help in his quest for wholeness is an Indian book, presented to him by his father, about "a Hindu saint who had visions" (*Darkness*, 153). Shawn is fascinated by the saint's description of his visions and behavior when he is in a trance. It is when Tran reads a passage of the book where the saint talks about his love for the youths who lived with him in the temple, a love inseparable from pain, that Shawn picks up a model for "saintly" behavior for himself. He perceives now that youths like him who have experienced broken homes, false declarations of love, and violence would, like the Hindu saint, have to walk his "world in boots and a trance" (*Darkness,* 157). When, however, he dresses up in his mother's clothes and puts on her makeup and then peers into an Indian immigrant home to spy on a small boy studying late at night, we begin to comprehend that in his search for wholeness Shawn had crossed over into the realm of the pathological. Without a doubt the most morbid tale collected in *Darkness,* "Saints" suggests clearly that failure to assimilate in one generation of immigrants can be a canker for another. Reading the story is a sobering process and confirms that, despite what Mukherjee claims in her Introduction, most of the American tales of *Darkness* are not about "the exuberance of immigration" and are not celebrations of immigration to the United States.

"The Imaginary Assassin," the penultimate piece collected in *Darkness,* is like "Saints" in having as its narrator a youth born in America of South Asian immigrant stock who is fascinated by stories of saintly figures from India. In this case, however, the narrator takes no part in the sequence of action described in the tale; his role is to first sketch in the background, then relate a tale he has heard from his grandfather about Gandhi, the most famous saintly figure in recent Indian history, and finally offer a kind of coda to the tale. From the background information provided by the narrator we gather that his family has settled in Yuba City, California, after his Sikh grandfather had made it his permanent home in 1948. We gather also that California had harbored illegal Sikh immigrants from the Punjab region of India for generations. These immigrants had come to the state to work in its farms after joining "the illegal alien's underground" (*Darkness,* 180). Gradually, these Sikhs had prospered in "paradise," although their children never took to studies or made the state's list of scholarship winners as did the children of Chinese and Japanese immigrant families. The narrator suggests that he has the potential to rival such scholarship winners but is too much of a romantic and too attracted to violence to either commit himself to higher studies or appreciate "the shabby diligence" of the immigrant lives that his family led in Yuba City. That is why he loves listening to the kind of story that his grandfather tells him one night when he is not yet 10 and that he retells for the reader in the central portion of his narrative.

His grandfather's story is of a man who had first come to California as a teenager before World War II and had stayed there for some time until he was arrested for shoplifting and then expelled from the country because he was discovered to be an illegal immigrant. According to his grandfather, on his return to India, he had assassinated Mahatama Gandhi, even though history records that he was shot to death at a public prayer meeting on 2 October 1948 by a Hindu fanatic. Evidently, he felt that he had to destroy the man who more than anyone was responsible for the partition of India, since partition also meant violent dislocations for Sikhs like him. Having shot Gandhi, the narrator's grandfather claims that he reentered California for a second time in 1948 and married into the Sikh community.

Are we to take the grandfather's claim to be Gandhi's assassin seriously or is it an entirely imaginary tale cooked up by a nearly senile old man for the benefit of his impressionable grandson? Certainly the comic and curious details of the story—for example, the bit about a woman on a train carrying the grandfather from Pakistan to India who wants to make love to him in front of a rail car full of refugees—suggest that we should not take him seriously at all and stick to the historical evidence. What, then, is Mukherjee's point in giving us an imaginary assassin of Gandhi who has settled in Yuba City, California? One possible explanation is that the story allows us to understand not only his "family's prodigality [which] expresses itself in slow, secretive ways" (*Darkness*, 190), but also the Sikh experience of diaspora, which led so many of them to eventually settle in North America and England. Additionally, "The Imaginary Assassin" allows us to understand the code of manly honor, an Indian version of machismo, which guides the conduct of some Sikh males everywhere.

In the coda of the tale, for instance, we get to see a replication of the grandfather's alleged act of violence in India when the narrator reports without comment that an illegal immigrant who had taken refuge in their house was arrested by Yuba City police the one night he left their basement because he had murdered another Sikh in Toronto. Also, Mukherjee appears to have written this tale, as she did "Saints," to portray the effect of the failure to assimilate in Indian families; it seems quite certain that the young narrator of the tale is going to be a failure in life as is his father because the grandfather carries in him a psychic wound and because these men have let nostalgia and false myths guide their lives. Finally, Mukherjee probably wrote "The Imaginary Assassin" out of her own fascination with the Sikh community, which would lead her to do research on their lives for the *The Sorrow and the Terror,* the book she co-authored with her husband two years after the publication of *Darkness.*

Stories such as "Saints" and the "Imaginary Assassins" are bravura pieces in that in them Mukherjee is writing about characters who are as removed from her own situation as is possible. Stories such as "The Lady from Lucknow" and "Visitors," on the other hand, have as their central reflectors the type of character Mukherjee has made uniquely her own: the restless Indian wife who would like to go beyond the confines of her marriage to embrace America but whose sexual adventure ends unsatis-factorily. What Peter Nazareth observes about *Wife* and "Visitors" could be applied with equal force to "The Lady from Lucknow": these are nar-ratives that deal "with the undermining in America of the myths and illusions about marriage with which an Indian woman is brought up" (Nazareth, 188).

Nafessa Hafez, the narrator of "The Lady from Lucknow," is a Muslim housewife who lives in Atlanta with her husband, Iqbal, and their two children. Iqbal works for IBM and is a decent man who has been able to give his wife and children a comfortable life. Nevertheless, he has certain preconceptions about the country he lives in; for example, he tells Nafessa that "Americans are crazy for sex." What he does not under-stand, however, is that Nafessa has had enough of being treated as an object that can be pushed around or as a person who can be taken for granted all the time, and is eager for the sexual freedom that America seems to offer, especially for someone like her who has been brought up in an extremely puritanical environment. Indeed, Iqbal has no idea that Nafessa is having an affair with James Beamish, a white American immunologist she met at a reception for international students at Emory University. Ironically, Iqbal had not attended the reception because he believed that such an event was "an excuse for looking back" to the land they had left many years ago when they should really be "looking for-ward," whereas Nafessa went because she always looked forward to whatever "was new and fascinating" (*Darkness*, 25).

Nafeesa's brief liaison with James ends abruptly soon after his wife discovers the adulterous pair in bed in the Beamish residence. What ran-kles Nafeesa is the way Kate Beamish decides to ignore her as someone beneath contempt, "someone without depth or color, a shadow-temptress who would float back to a city of teeming millions when the affair with James had ended" (*Darkness*, 33). It was as if Kate was a *mem-sahib* in some colonial outpost, indulging her husband's tastes for a col-ored mistress whom he would abandon sooner or later. What Nafeesa perceives, then, is that she had merely substituted the traditional male master of her own culture with an American one. Nafeesa, therefore,

should feel humiliated at the way what began "as an adventure has
become shabby and complex" (*Darkness,* 33). But her spirit is too
resilient and her attitude to her life too complex to leave her feeling shattered. "The Lady from Lucknow" thus ends ambivalently; Nafessa is still
attracted to James Beamish and almost wants to respond to his renewed
overtures, but also feels too pained and broken-hearted to pick up the
threads of her affair with him. As she sees it, she seems someone forever
destined to be caught in a bind: "I have lived a life perched on the edge
of ripeness and decay. The traveller feels at home everywhere, because
she is never at home anywhere" (*Darkness,* 31).

But if an American male has failed Nafeesa, America itself has a positive charge for Mukherjee in that the country offers sexual freedom and,
by implication, freedom from all stifling conventions. As Liew-Geok
Leong observes, "The seduction exercised by a more open and anarchic
environment and the liberation of sensibility, if only partial at times, are
particularly evident in Mukherjee's women" (Leong, 495). Although
Leong does not mention her, Vinita, the 25-year-old protagonist of
"Visitors," is one such woman. Typically, she has been brought over from
Calcutta to play the role of the conventional Indian wife. Her husband,
Sailen Kumar, is, once again typically, a decent and successful but somewhat complacent man. Like Iqbal, he does not realize that though she is
happy with the material prosperity of their lives, she feels unfulfilled.
While he is content to remain within the conventions of his community,
she secretly hopes for something or someone that will disrupt her life.
Not unlike Dimple in *Wife,* she is ready to change herself in America
because "she is now cut off from her moorings" (*Darkness,* 166) and
excited to be "in a new country with no rules" (*Darkness,* 167).

How much Vinita has been changed by America becomes obvious
when one day she has a visitor drop in without notice at her apartment.
He is Rajiv Khanna, a graduate student at Columbia, who has ostensibly
come to invite her to a classical Indian dance concert being held on campus but is really planning to seduce her. Although he has been brought
up in America, Khanna appears to have retained his Indianness and
seems nervous and unsure of himself (as we have seen in *Wife,* the South
Asian men in Mukherjee's fiction never aim at total assimilation, unlike
the women). Vinita does not know how to react to this unexpected visitor; she is flattered by his attention and does not want him to leave; on
the other hand, she is only too aware of the impropriety of receiving a
man she hardly knows when her husband is away. When he blurts out
that she is the goddess of his dreams and that he had been wanting her

ever since he first saw her, she realizes that she is not as shocked as she should be. On the contrary, seeing before her a man "unmoored by passion," she thinks, "We are both a new breed, testing new feelings in new battlegrounds" (*Darkness,* 172). And yet when he tries to grab her, she resists and feels overcome with shame. Frustrated, Khanna leaves, not perceiving that he has left behind a thoroughly aroused woman.

As "Visitors" concludes, Vinita is shown to be restless and over-whelmed by the desire to break free from the "haven" provided for her by her husband and to "run off into the alien American night where only shame and disaster can await her" (*Darkness,* 176). As was the case with Nafessa, the lady from Lucknow, Vinita seems ready to fly away from the gilded cage she had been living in, and yet there seems to be no safe destination in sight for her. Nafeesa and Vinita appear to be only somewhat better placed than Dimple, who had reached a dead end and had found no way out of her bind except by killing her husband. Significantly, "Visitors" ends with a question mark; Vinita's fate is thus left uncertain, but at least Mukherjee has moved her heroine beyond madness to at least the possibility of a "liberation of sensibility" that Leong has discerned in her fiction. Or, as Patricia Bradbury puts it in her review of *Darkness,* Mukherjee is showing in such stories "identities slowly breaking into pieces, cracked open by raw and totally alien dreams," but there is always "the unstated promise" in them that "identities in new and unimaginable modes will soon be rebuilt again" (Bradbury, 43).

Angela, the titular character of the first story of *Darkness,* has a surer knowledge of where she should be going even though she is indelibly scarred by the physical and emotional wounds she had received as a six-year-old brutalized by Pakistani soldiers attempting to prevent the birth of Bangladesh in 1971. Thus, although Angela remembers throughout the narrative the violence done to her and her country by the soldiers, significantly, these memories flood her consciousness at the end only when she considers the possibility of marriage to Dr. Menezies, the middle-aged Indian doctor who is part of her Iowa circle of acquaintances. Dr. Menezies is a considerate and earnest man, but Angela resists the thought of marriage to him despite the sense of security he can give her as a husband and despite their common origins in "the hunger and misery of the subcontinent" (*Darkness,* 8).

What Dr. Menezies does not understand is that Angela's experience of war, orphan homes, adoption by an American family, and a major automobile accident that has spared her but left her adopted sister Delia in a critical condition has made her conclude that her life is full of mar-

vels and that she has a special mission in life to carry out. She is grateful
for the attention Dr. Menezies pays her; nevertheless, she is sure she
should "wait for some sign" and has "been saved for a purpose"
(*Darkness*, 19). Mrs. Grimlund, the nurse who is looking after Delia in
the hospital, is percipient when she notes how strong Angela really is.
"Angela" is, in essence, the tale of a survivor who seems destined to
retain her independence and go her own way in life. If the horrible memories of the past come to her mind at the conclusion, they do so only as
a kind of defense mechanism to warn her against any action such as marriage to Dr. Menezies, which will reconnect her to the land she had to
leave.

Angela, in other words, has willed herself to accept America,
although she will carry unpleasant fragments of the past forever in her
memory. "Hindus," the seventh story of *Darkness*, is also about a woman
who endeavors to embrace America but who finds that she cannot completely escape the past. Leela, the protagonist of this story, strives for a
long time to move farther and farther away from her origins but
becomes conscious at the end of her narrative that "no matter how passionately we link bodies with our new countries, we never escape the
early days" (*Darkness*, 139).

Leela's consciousness of her inescapable difference from other
Americans is thus some time in coming. When we first encounter her,
Leela is in New York visiting an art gallery of Islamic miniatures from
India at the urging of Derek, her liberal-minded filmmaker husband.
There they meet Pat, a family friend of Leela's whom she had last seen in
Calcutta at least nine years ago. In these nine years Leela, like her creator
a beautiful Bengali Brahmin, has, again like Mukherjee, left the privi-
leged life she had led in Calcutta, moved to North America, broken caste,
and married a Canadian. Meanwhile, Pat, really Maharajah Patwant
Singh, has, as his calling card announces, become a "purveyor and
exporter" of Indian antiques. Leela, too, has shortened her name (she was
Leelah in India), reminding us of the transformations and the shedding of
old selves that go on in the New World. But while Pat has maintained at
least a business connection with India—hustling his family heirlooms in
America—Leela has come to the point where she asserts her American
citizenship and "disclaim[s] any recent connection with India" (*Darkness*,
133). Not that she has cut herself loose from India out of a sense of outrage at the changes going on there, as does the aristocratic Pat; her attitude, she avers, is a practical one: "India teaches her children; you have
seen the worst. Now go out and don't be afraid" (*Darkness*, 135).

As the narrative proceeds, we see Leela distancing herself even more from India after she has separated from her husband and taken a job as an administrative assistant in a New York publishing house. By this time the city has become for her "a vast sea in which new Americans like myself could disappear and resurface at will" (*Darkness*, 136). When she meets Pat again one day in her office where he has come to discuss the book he is going to write for her boss about his memories of princely India—he is still hustling his Indian bric-a-brac in America—she has lost her Indian accent and in her Western clothes looks indistinguishable from any other American woman. Surprised to hear her speak in Hindi with Pat, one of her colleagues remarks that she had no idea that Leela spoke "Hindu." But Leela has no intention of correcting her colleague's confusion between Hindu and Hindi. What strikes her then with something of the force of a Joycean epiphany in her story is that "no matter what language I speak it will come out slightly foreign, no matter how perfectly I mouth it. There's a whole world of us now, speaking Hindu" (*Darkness*, 140).

This revelation highlights Leela's ambivalence about her status in America: on the one hand, it expresses a sense of defiance ("There's a whole world of us now, speaking Hindu") and registers a consciousness of the demographic changes taking place in the United States because of a rush of immigrants from Asia; on the other, it articulates a sense of resignation at the thought that she would always be perceived as "slightly foreign." "Hindus," therefore, captures perfectly the ambivalent mood in which even the American tales of *Darkness* were written; despite the exuberant Introduction to the book, the most optimistic voice that Mukherjee can muster in its stories is Leela's characterization of herself at the end of the tale as a "blind and groping conquistador who had come to the New World too late" (*Darkness*, 141).

There is a note of ambivalence, too, in "Courtly Vision," the last piece of *Darkness*. "Courtly Vision" purports to be a five-page exposition of a Mugal painting, *Emperor on Horseback Leaves Walled City*, being sold for $750 at an auction like the one at Sotheby's that Derek and Leela are visiting at the beginning of "Hindus" with a catalog of Islamic miniature paintings in their hands. What Mukherjee is attempting in this tale, however, is nothing less than a statement of her artistic credo at this point in her career. The ridiculously undervalued painting of the great Mugal emperor Akbar leaving his dream city of Fatehpur Sikri is a metaphor for Mukherjee's style in *Darkness*, for, like the painting— which depicts treachery and deception in a world that is supposed to be ordered and free from subterfuge—Mukherjee has shown in her 11 tales the unpleasant truths about immigrant lives in a land that was supposed to be a haven for all immigrants. What the emperor in the painting wants from his court painter—*"total vision," "infinite vistas" (Darkness,* 199), the whole truth about the present and insight into the future (even if this means depicting the impending doom of his city), sorrow and laughter ("Tell me who to fear and who to kill but tell it to me in a way that makes me smile")—was what Mukherjee had set as her goals in writing these stories.

In his appreciative *Canadian Literature* essay on *Darkness,* Peter Nazareth concludes that "Courtly Vision" offers us the terms in which we must praise the book: like Akbar's court painter, "this is what the literary artist has done: she has penetrated below the surface, found the reality, and told the truth on several grains of rice." But as a writer-artist, Mukherjee, asserts Nazareth, goes beyond the "two-dimensional" surface of "Courtly Vision" to portray the immigrant's "complex, multicultural world"—a world containing much bad news as well as considerable potential (Nazareth, 190). Reviewing *Darkness* in the *New York Times Book Review,* Hope Cooke comments that "Courtly Vision" "provides through the study of a Mogul painting insights into the intricacies of the author's own miniaturist writing."[16] A more complex reading of "Courtly Vision" and the clues it offers to a reader of *Darkness* is Gita Rajan's; she argues that "the painting's miniaturized texture could also be read as Janus-faced" and that Mukherjee is "stylizing the reader's gaze; like the Mogul emperor who is glancing back into treachery and deceit and forward into an exquisitely ordered world, so, too, the immigrant can walk away from disillusionment and look forward with hope into the new future-land" (Rajan, 238).

A reader of "Courtly Vision," therefore, can come away from this piece with insights into the technique as well as the theme Mukherjee adopts for *Darkness.* As the concluding piece suggests, the stories of the volume have a style that depends on suggestive details, wide vistas, and ambivalence. But if Mukherjee has gone back to an Indian painting tradition for metaphors for her technique, she has also used the resources of contemporary American prose to convey her theme. As Mukherjee has pointed out in her 1988 *Massachusetts Review* interview, by the time she wrote *Darkness* she had "adopted American English" as her language (649). Shawn Patel, for example, speaks perfectly in the idiom of the contemporary American teenager and in the tradition of a Holden Caufield. Mukherjee claims in the Introduction to the volume that she can hear America singing and invokes Whitman as a predecessor; certainly she is following him and Mark Twain in her experiments with the American spoken voice in fiction. It is also a voice that is bolder, emphatic, and more direct, and a lot less ironic and sarcastic than it used to be. True, Mukherjee will still revert to the knowing narrative voice and the superior tone she had adopted in her first two novels in a story such as "A Father," but it is surely significant that she is now more often than not ready to abandon omniscience and adopt the voice of the new immigrants in a gesture of solidarity with them.

Ironically, however, a book that strove so hard to be in the American tradition and that contained bitter reflections on Canadian society was actually published in Canada after a number of American publishers had rejected the manuscript. Mukherjee reports in her 1990 *Iowa Review* interview how only 600 copies were imported into America by Penguin Books and how these copies disappeared soon. Even after the book went out of print fairly quickly, no attempt was made to reprint the book in the country for a while (27). Evidently American publishers had not caught on in 1985 to the relevance of the book to the demographic changes in the American landscape and the revaluations of American attitudes toward race, ethnicity, and gender that were going on in the American academy. Evidently, too, American publishers had not noticed the enthusiastic review of the book by Hope Cooke that appeared in the *New York Times Book Review* on 12 January 1986.

Ironically, also, *Darkness* was quite favorably received in Canada. In what surely is a tribute to the spirit of multiculturalism that Mukherjee derides in her work, George Woodcock, one of the elder statesmen of Canadian letters, welcomed the volume despite its bitterness against Canada and regrets her move to the United States as a loss for his country's literature. Wryly noting "the relief and gladness" with which Mukherjee immersed herself "in the melting pot, which many of us have not found so welcoming," Woodcock points out that she had won major awards in Canada for her work and that a story such as "Tamurlane" clearly illustrates the way "the conflict of Canada" has stimulated Mukherjee into producing the best stories of the collection.[17]

But perhaps the subtlest review of *Darkness* was that written by Anita Desai, the other Indian woman novelist writing in English to have achieved international recognition in recent years. Desai is quite generous in praising the collection; she appreciates Mukherjee's ability to catch with "near-perfection the American tone, the American hysteria, the American *angst*" in some stories, and she is complimentary of "the ironic tone, just edged with bitterness, her sharpness of observation, the elegance of both her style and her attitude, somewhat world-weary and cynical, with an undercurrent of genuine pain" in some other tales. Desai is also percipient, however, in questioning Mukherjee's claim to have always written herself into her immigrants' lives. Probing Mukherjee's claim that she had embraced the new immigrants from South Asia in her tales, Desai detects a degree of detachment and even suggests that the storyteller is "perhaps too detached" from her characters in a story such as "A Father." On the other hand, Desai indicts stories such as "Nostalgia" or "Visitors" for "lacking both weight and shape and betraying somewhat repellent vanity and self-indulgence"; in other words, Mukherjee has not detached herself sufficiently from her protagonists in these tales. Desai also questions Mukherjee's claim to have followed in Malamud's footsteps; in Desai's view, the South Asian American's "material is not so tractable, not so acccessible to universal tones and simply not in the same class of human tragedy as that to which the Jewish characters" of the great American storyteller belongs. Nevertheless, Desai ends her thoughtful review by conceding Mukherjee's talent and praising the achievement of *Darkness*. What Desai says in the final line of her evaluation can also be utilized to conclude this discussion of the book: "What Bharati Mukherjee has done, and done admirably, is to stand witness, with honesty, with clear-sightedness and with remarkable distinction" to the experience of Indian immigrants in the North America of the 1980s (Desai, 144–46).

The Sorrow and the Terror

No sooner had Bharati Mukherjee completed *Darkness* than she began work on another collection of stories about Asian immigrants in North America. By this time she was bursting with such tales of immigrant lives. Getting an NEA grant helped her write these tales, as did a semester off from teaching. As a result, she was able to complete quite a few stories in an eight-month period. But before she could write enough of them to fill a volume, her attention was diverted by the events surrounding the 23 June 1985 crash of an Air India jet over Ireland that killed 329 people, mostly Canadian citizens of South Asian origin. Terrorists belonging to the Sikh community claimed responsibility for the disaster; evidently, they had planted a bomb on the Air India plane in a bid to draw attention to their campaign to create Khalistan. This was to be an independent country for their community to be carved out of Punjab, the Indian state where Sikhs constituted a majority of the population. Although Mukherjee and her husband had been in the United States for over five years at this time, they had still not lost interest in Canada or the South Asian expatriate communities in that country. Moreover, as the Canadian tales of *Darkness* reveal, Mukherjee continued to be peeved by her memories of the indignities she had suffered there, and it seemed to her now that the plane crash probably originated from the same flaws in Canadian immigration policy that had led to the racist incidents she had endured, witnessed, or heard about in Toronto and Montreal.

The Sorrow and the Terror: The Haunting Legacy of the Air India Tragedy (1987), the second of the two nonfiction books Mukherjee co-wrote with her husband, Clark Blaise, is the result of a painstaking investigation carried out by the couple into the circumstances that led to the plane crash and the immediate consequences of this major air disaster. Husband and wife began work on their project in January 1986. Using their weekend breaks, their two-member investigative team would drive to Toronto to talk to the families of the crash victims, to Canadian police officials, aviation experts, and to anyone else involved who was willing to be interviewed for the book. They also visited Montreal, Ottawa, and Detroit. The couple flew to Vancouver a number of times, since the Khalistan movement drew mostly on the large concentration of Sikhs in the west coast of Canada. On weekends when they stayed back in New York where they were both teaching at that time, they would mingle with the many Sikhs in the state and investigate the workings of the Sikh organization that acted as a front for the Khalistan terrorists. Mukherjee and Blaise also took time out from their teaching to gain access to Canadian government files on the Air India disaster and to attend the trials for compensation that began afterwards in New York and Toronto. They read newspaper reports, trial transcripts, and government accounts. In addition, they took a trip to Ireland to be present in a ceremony where a memorial for the crash victims sponsored by the Irish, Canadian, and Indian governments was unveiled in a formal ceremony.

Unlike *Days and Nights in Calcutta,* basically a compilation of separate records they had kept during their sabbatical year in Calcutta, *The Sorrow and the Terror* is thus a genuinely collaborative work. This is how Mukherjee describes the process of her collaboration with Blaise: "Clark had done some of the interviews. I had done some myself, and we had done some together. We had an enormous amount of material which we then parcelled off into different parts to do the first draft. Then we edited.

I edited his, he edited mine. Every single word was somehow approved by both writers" (1990 interview, 14). Afterwards they went over the manuscript line by line with their publisher's lawyer to ensure that the book did not become the target for libel suits. Finally, and because of a year's sustained work, the book was ready for publication.

What drove Mukherjee and Blaise to go through such labors, and what made them put aside their creative work for such a long time to produce a book on a plane crash that everyone else, except the families of the victims, seemed only too eager to forget? The first sentence of *The Sorrow and the Terror* emphasizes the compulsive nature of the couple's project; they were "driven to write this book," they declare, "as citizens bearing witness." The Air India disaster, they were convinced, was "fundamentally an immigration tragedy with terrorist overtones."[18] Of course, the Canadian government took the line that the plane disaster was the consequence of sectarian problems in India, and of course the Indian government seemed content to treat the crash as something that had happened overseas due to circumstances beyond its control. Nevertheless, Mukherjee and Blaise are certain that the real reason for the Air India disaster was Canada's "problematic policy of multiculturalism itself, the nation's desire to preserve and even foster ethnic diversity" (*Sorrow*, x). From this perspective, the couple argue, the plane crash was "a long time in the making" and not merely the result of Sikh desire to take revenge on India's brutal attempts to throttle the Khalistan movement. What husband and wife wanted also to drive home to Canadians was that the Air India disaster was "an intimate tragedy with implications for everyone" in the country (*Sorrow*, xii). They hoped, too, that their book would be a way of remembering the lives lost when the plane went down over Ireland because of the terrorist bomb, and would help avoid disasters caused by misguided immigration policies in the future.

Chapter 4 of *The Sorrow and the Terror* explains specifically why Mukherjee and Blaise viewed Canadian government policy to be the ultimate cause of the Air India disaster. According to the authors, because of its "complacency" and because it treated "multiculturalism not as an ideal, but as an expedient" (*Sorrow*, 199), the Canadian government had let the tragedy happen. They emphasize that the Canadian authorities knew of the existence of terrorist cells and were aware of the policies the terrorists were advocating and the course of action they were preparing themselves for. And yet because of the policy of multiculturalism that the authors considered tantamount to doing nothing for Canada's "non-French, non-English 'ethnics' and 'visible minorities,'" the Canadian police had looked the other way while the Khalistanis had fomented their plot to bomb an Air India flight. As the authors put it, "many of the grieving Air India families and many anti-Khalistani Sikhs wonder why their requests for government review of slanderous broadcasts and libelous editorials in Canada's Punjabi-language media, of death threats and even assaults were not followed up" (*Sorrow*, 201). Apparently, Canadian intelligence apparatus knew also that the Sikh terrorists were acquiring the capacity to assemble bombs, but structural flaws in the law-enforcement agencies prevented them from intervening until it was too late. But as far as Blaise and Mukherjee are concerned, more than anything else, the terrorist cells were not taken to task because of what they label as "a national character flaw: the myth of instinctive goodness" that led the security officials to conclude that "it can't happen here" (*Sorrow*, 203).

Mukherjee and Blaise continue to put Canada's policy of multiculturalism on the rack in their account of the consequences of the Air India disaster. They point out that although most of the people who died in the crash were Canadian citizens, the Canadian establishment took the policy of citing the dead as members of the "Indo-Canadian community." Multiculturalism, in the authors' views, meant treating the dead as "not-quite Canadians" and was another way of perpetuating the racist distinction betweem "them" and "us."

The Sorrow and the Terror contains a comprehensive indictment of Canadian attitude toward immigrants from South Asia. To quote the authors, "Canada contributed more to the tragedy than it has ever acknowledged" (*Sorrow*, 204). Although Mukherjee and Blaise strive to adopt an objective tone and attempt to give a balanced view of the Air India plane crash and its aftermath, it is difficult not to see their account as somehow tinged with their own personal experience of the pain inflicted by Canada's policy of multiculturalism. After all, had not Mukherjee and Blaise left the security of their tenured jobs and the respect the two had earned in academic and artistic circles in Canada because of her firsthand knowledge of racism on Toronto streets? The bitterness and the anger that had driven Mukherjee to attack covert and overt racism in Canada in "An Invisible Woman" and in the Introduction and the "Canadian" tales of *Darkness* also inspired her to team up with her husband in tracking the origins and the legacy of the Air India tragedy.

The Sorrow and the Terror thus has its place in any treatment of the "Canadian" phase of Mukherjee's literary career. Although the book is the least talked about of her works, it should be read if only because it helps us to fully understand her indignant rejection of Canadian immigration policy and her enthusiastic embrace of America's melting-pot approach to its new immigrants. The book also rounds off one phase of her work, for, with one important exception, she would stop writing about Canada directly or indirectly from now on and would devote herself to writing about American settings and situations. The one exception, of course, is the story "The Management of Grief," which she included as the concluding tale of *The Middleman and Other Stories*. This story grew directly out of her research into the Air India disaster and deals with the effort by someone affected by the plane crash to get on with her life. But as we shall see in the next chapter, its optimistic conclusion makes it a story Mukherjeee could have written only in the American phase of her career, after all the bitterness in her about Canada had been replaced by hope about the possibilities of rerooting herself in the United States.

Chapter Four
The Exuberance of Immigration

If the tone of the work Bharati Mukherjee did on her experience of the aloofness of expatriation in Canada is set by her indignant essay "An Invisible Woman," the mood of the fiction she produced after she became an American citizen is captured perfectly in her exuberant essay "Immigrant Writing: Give Us Your Maximalists!" Published in the 28 August 1988 *New York Times Book Review,* this piece records Mukherjee's excitement about the ceremony in a Federal District Court House in Manhattan that February that made her a citizen of the United States. Eight years after she and her family left Canada in frustration at that country's policy of multiculturalism, Mukherjee is clearly delighted by the prospects awaiting her now that she had formally cast herself into America's melting pot culture. But Mukherjee is more than effervescent in this piece; she is also registering in it her intention to transform American literature by including in it the stories of people like her who were bringing new life through immigration to what could otherwise have been a jaded landscape.

The essay's opening line—"I'm one of you now"—boldly echoes Walt Whitman's basic ploy in "Song of Myself." What she has assumed that her American readers should assume, Mukherjee seems to be saying, is that in celebrating her citizenship ceremony she was celebrating the spirit that has always thrust America forward. America, to Whitman, was fluid, dynamic. Mukherjee, too, sees all around her "the face of America changing." And just as Whitman had arrogated the right to speak for all Americans, she presumes in the essay to speak for "the new Americans from nontraditional immigrant countries" altering America yet again ("Maximalists," 1). "Such energy, such comedy, such sophistication and struggle and hunger to belong"—how could she not seize on such material for her work? The new immigrants were "bursting with stories" ("Maximalists," 28) about discarded pasts and time travel and eager to embrace the present. For her part, she could do no better than to transmit their stories by entering their lives and by taking advantage of her "history-mandated training in seeing myself as the 'other'" ("Maximalists," 29).[1]

The Middleman and Other Stories (1988) and *Jasmine* (1989) celebrate the new immigrants and narrate the stories they were bursting with. Expanding her range in these works to articulate the lives of Americans who had made their way to the country from Asia, Africa, and the West Indies in the last two decades or so, Mukherjee ventures to fill them with exuberant tales of immigration, with surprising stories of the clash of cultures, and with fascinating portraits of people in transit or caught in the middle or split between an old world and a new one.

The Middleman and *Jasmine* thus represent a distinctive phase in Mukherjee's literary career. Although her theme remains migrant lives, the angle of vision has changed radically. In most of the stories collected in *The Middleman* and in her third novel Mukherjee eschews the omniscient/superior perspective she had adopted earlier and attempts to allow her new Americans to tell their own stories. Occasionally, she even looks at them from the point of view of white and "old" Americans. The writing is altogether more flexible, the idiom distinctively American, the tone no longer ironic or bitter. Her characters now are seen to be emerging from shadowy or marginal lives and putting out feelers to root themselves in a brave new world.

Throughout *The Middleman* and *Jasmine,* then, Mukherjee is involved in presenting immigration from the Third World to North America as a "process of uprooting and rerooting" (1988 interview, 648). Published within a span of 18 months, these two works of fiction and "Immigrant Writing" illustrate that Mukherjee's theme in this phase of her literary career has become "the making of new Americans" ("Woman," 26). Ideally, one imagines, Mukherjee would like her readers to view them in the way she feels a Mughal miniature painting should be seen—simultaneously, so that one gets "the sense of the interpenetration of all things" ("Woman," 26). This chapter, however, focuses first on *The Middleman* and then on *Jasmine* as Mukherjee moves decisively away from the "darkness" phase of her writing, where she dealt with expatriates trying to preserve their identities in a hostile world, to immigrants striving to transform their identities and stake out their claims to America.

The Middleman and Other Stories

Bharati Mukherjee has said that the stories of *The Middleman* came to her in two "intense flurries," although she had been contemplating writing the volume for some time (1988 interview, 647). She had, in fact, begun work on one cycle of stories as soon as she had finished the tales collected in *Darkness* in 1985 and had got a semester off from teaching because of an NEA grant. Then she became intensely involved in *The Sorrow and the Terror,* the book she wrote with her husband to trace the events leading to the 1985 Air India crash over Ireland and to draw out the implications of what she perceived to be a disaster caused at least in part by Canada's policy of multiculturalism. As soon as this book was completed she wrote some more stories for *The Middleman* in the summer of 1987. Certainly not by a coincidence, the volume was published in New York only a couple of months after she became an American citizen in February 1988.

Mukherjee has identified the theme of the stories collected in *The Middleman* as "the new, changing America" (1988 interview, 648). America, in her view, was changing decisively recently because of large-scale immigration to the country from the Third World. The arrival of nontraditional immigrants was also having an impact on older Americans, just as the new breed of immigrants were themselves being altered by their contact with a distinctively different culture and ethos. Responding specifically to a question from the interviewer about what was special about this collection of her stories, Mukherjee says that she was writing "about well-known American establishments such as the family, in a unique way" and in a distinctly American idiom (1988 interview, 648). As far as she could see, her American families are different from those treated by other American writers in their fiction. What is more, she was bent on showing that "the American family has become very different, not just because of social influences and new sexual standards, but because of the interaction between mainstream Americans and new immigrants" (1988 interview, 649).

By the time Mukherjee came to write *The Middleman* she had finally got over the dark mood that had engulfed her in Canada and that had stayed with her for a long time even after she returned to the United States in 1980. Consequently, the woman writing this volume is confident and optimistic, having a clear sense of being where she wanted to be: although she was still "moving in degrees of acculturation, the overall authorial vision" had become much more "consistent" (1990 interview, 28). It is no doubt because of her newfound confidence in her mission as a writer that Mukherjee has greatly expanded her range of characters, settings, and narrative perspectives in these stories to articulate her vision of the "new, changing America." Only occasionally does she use a woman as a central reflector or depend on protagonists of South Asian origin, as was the case in her *Darkness* tales. Indeed, she now

seems to be even going out of her way to draw on characters from relatively peripheral areas who have had diasporic experiences. Also, she
appears in this volume to delight in putting her protagonists in extreme
situations.

The first-person narrator and central character of the first and titular
story of the collection, "The Middleman," for instance, is Alfie Judah, a
professional gunman originally from Iraq. The next story of the collection, "A Wife's Story," returns us to Mukherjee's favorite narrator, an
Indian wife in North America about to break loose from her kind. "Loose
Ends," the third tale, is told from the point of view of Jeb Marshall, a
Vietnam veteran scarred by his experience of war. He is succeeded as a
narrator in "Orbiting" by Renata de Marcos, a second-generation
American woman of Italian-Spanish origins who is dating an Afghan
man. "Fighting for the Rebound," the fifth piece, has as its central reflector another American, identified only as Griff, who is being asked to
commit himself to his Filipino girlfriend, Blanquita. While "The Tenant,"
the first piece of the volume presented by an omniscient narrator, takes
us back to familiar Mukherjee territory—a Bengali woman adrift in
America—"Fathering," the sixth tale, is a story presented by another
Vietnam veteran who is having to choose between the claims made on
him by his half-Vietnamese daughter and his white American common-
law wife. It is followed by "Jasmine," a story presented from an omniscient perspective but centering on a Trinidadian Indian teenager who is
savoring the United States for the first time. "Danny's Girls," the eighth
tale, records the consequences of the infatuation of its unnamed narrator,
an Indian teenager who has come to America with his family from
Uganda, with a Nepalese woman "imported" into America as a mail-
order bride. In "Buried Lives," the third of the three narratives of the collection presented from an omniscient perspective, Mukherjee traces the
peregrinations of Mr. Venkatesan, a Tamil from Sri Lanka bent on
migrating to Canada. "The Management of Grief," the last story, is about
Mrs. Bhave, an Indo-Canadian who tries to cope with the loss of her family in a plane crash.

Mukherjee's expanded range and confidence in her ability to write
about old and new Americans being transformed by nontraditional
immigration patterns can also be seen in her choice of settings and in
her use of time in her tales. Except for "Buried Lives"—which follows
Mr. Venkatesan for some months as he takes the underground route
favored by Sri Lankan Tamils fleeing from the turmoil in their country

to the West and ends in Hamburg—all the stories of *The Middleman* seem to be deliberately set all over North America to prove how the entire continent was being transformed by the influx of immigrants of Asian origin. The title story, for example, has Alfie Judah plying his trade as a middleman and, typically for him, living dangerously for a couple of days in a Central American republic. "A Wife's Story" follows Panna Bhatt for a few weeks in New York City. "Loose Ends" makes good use of a southern Florida landscape being taken over by Asian and Hispanic immigrants. It is very much Mukherjee's point in this story that its protagonist, Jeb Marshall, stalks the area but cannot connect with it or its new residents. A Thanksgiving Day dinner in New York City is the setting of "Orbiting." "Fighting for the Rebound" takes us for a few days to the world of yuppies, condominiums, and malls in fast-changing Atlanta. No doubt as a deliberate contrast, the slow-paced "The Tenant" is set for the most part in the small town of Cedar Falls, Iowa. The action of the tightly controlled story "Fathering" takes place in the town of Rock Springs, somewhere in upstate New York, and does not take more than a few hours. "Jasmine" begins dramatically at a border crossing in Michigan and shows the protagonist gradually settling down in Ann Arbor after she has successfully managed to enter the United States as an illegal immigrant. In "Danny's Girls" we become aware of the large Indian presence in the New York City borough of Queens. "The Management of Grief" follows Mrs. Bhave from Toronto to Ireland to India and back to Toronto again. Slowly we see her coming to terms with the loss of her husband and son in the plane crash.

Although Mukherjee manages to assemble such a diverse gallery of characters from almost half the globe and makes use of such disparate settings in *The Middleman,* and although her basic theme in all but two of the stories ("Buried Lives" and "The Management of Grief") is the impact of the United States on its new immigrants and the effect they were having on older Americans, the stories can be conveniently divided into four different groups. In the first group are "The Management of Grief," "A Wife's Story," and "The Tenant." These are narratives with the types of protagonists who have most frequented Mukherjee's previous fiction: Indian women who are having to cope with life in North America. The second group consists of "The Middleman," "Danny's Girls," "Jasmine," and "Buried Lives." The protagonists of these stories either inhabit the shadowy world of illegal immigrants or are involved in disreputable actions. In the third group are "Loose Ends" and "Fighting for the Rebound," two tales of white Americans who, for different reasons, cannot or do not want to connect with the new Americans in their midst. The two stories in the final group, "Orbiting" and "Fathering," are also about the response of white Americans to people from cultures once considered alien. Only in these two stories do the older Americans respond positively to the demands made on their emotions by the new Americans.

"The Management of Grief" is not inappropriately the last story of *The Middleman,* but it is a good place to begin a discussion of the volume because it is in some ways a transitional work, bridging the world of *Darkness* with that of *The Middleman.* This is because Mrs. Bhave's calm account of the depression and numbness that sets upon her after the loss of her family in the Air India crash and the details of the disaster seem to have grown directly out of the mood that made Mukherjee write *Darkness* and *The Sorrow and the Terror.* In doing her research for the latter book, Mukherjee appears to have come up with the idea of "The Management of Grief." As in the book, Mukherjee fills in her tale with details of the pathos of survival and underscores the inadequacy of Canadian officialdom faced with the relatives of the crash victims. In fact, the bureaucratic Judith Templeton who calls on Mrs. Bhave and the other relatives in "The Management of Grief" has a distinct resemblance to Ann Vane, the white Canadian social worker in "Isolated Incidents," one of the more memorable stories of *Darkness.* Like Ann, who works in a Human Rights Office without being able to solace her clients or understand their predicaments, Judith is basically well-meaning but ultimately ill-equipped to "manage" the grief of the Indo-Canadian community because of the cultural distance separating her from them.

But if Mukherjee is unremitting in her attacks on Canadian official policy toward its Asian migrants, "The Management of Grief" concludes in a manner that leaves no doubt that it belongs rightfully to *The Middleman* and not to *Darkness.* This is because her moving narrative shows Mrs. Bhave going beyond the stage where she had to endure futile private or public attempts at consolation in Canada and had to make do with antidepressants. When she returns to India to find comfort in her family and gets reacquainted with Indian ways of "managing grief," she enters for a time the zone inhabited by other middlemen and -women of the collection. As she puts it, "I am trapped between two modes of knowledge. . . . I flutter between worlds."[2] Soon she realizes that she cannot get the consolation she seeks in the country of her origin. Shaila

Bhave, therefore, returns to Toronto. Here, in a vision, she hears the voices of her family urging her to "*go, be brave*" (*Middleman,* 194). Like Ursula Brangwen's sighting of the rainbow at the end of her quest for fulfillment in Lawrence's *The Rainbow,* the voices she hears tell her to be intrepid, to avoid compromise, and to, in effect, go beyond the "middle state." That is why "The Management of Grief" is rightly the story that concludes *The Middleman,* even though it can also be considered, as it has been here, a work that links it to her previous work.

"A Wife's Story" reminds us of Mukherjee's second novel and of stories such as "The Lady from Lucknow" and "Visitors" from *Darkness.* As in those earlier narratives, Mukherjee here focuses on an Indian wife who is willing to immerse herself in the life and the mores of urban America but who is also being pulled back, at least for the time being, by her Indianness. In other words, the Panna Bhatt we see at first is the typical Mukherjee protagonist, caught in the middle. When she begins her account, for instance, Panna is in a New York theater with Imre, a fellow international graduate student with whom she is intimate and who is her date for the night. The play being staged in the theater is by David Mamet and is full of Patel jokes. Panna feels only too conscious of the way the jokes stereotype Indians (just as she remembers the manner in which Steven Spielberg misrepresents Indian eating habits in one of his Indiana Jones films). The fact that there are Patel jokes in a New York play is a sure sign, however, that Indian immigrants have become part of America's psyche, for here in America "insults . . . is a kind of acceptance." Nevertheless, she cannot help being upset in the theater at a culture that makes her kind a butt of its comics and refuses them "instant dignity." Later, however, she rationalizes, "We've made it. Patels must have made it. Mamet, Spielberg: they're not condescending to us. Maybe they're a little bit afraid" (*Middleman,* 28). She concedes that "she "know[s] how both sides feel, [and] that's the trouble" (*Middleman,* 26).

Panna is in the United States studying for a Ph.D. in special education while her husband is staying back in India working as a vice president in a textile mill. Partially liberated, well-bred, and increasingly displaced, Panna knows she has drifted away considerably from her considerate but tradition-conscious husband. All this becomes obvious in a cameo scene when she hugs Imre impulsively on Broadway after the play. As it occurs to her then, she hugs him because she is too shy to dance with him in the street as she feels like doing. But then, she realizes, her husband would "never dance or hug a woman on Broadway"

(*Middleman,* 27). Always she is reminded of the physical and emotional distance she has traveled. Just as she thinks instinctively of her husband when she hugs Imre, she is reminded of "destitutes" in Indian streets when she looks at "the hordes of New York street people" (*Middleman,* 27). When she sees Eric, her roommate Charity Chin's lover, sneak his hand under the Chinese girl's sweater, what flashes through Panna's mind is how Charity's figure has made her "a model with high ambitions," whereas in India "she'd be a flat-chested old maid!" (29). No question that in the two years that she has been on her own in America "she has broadened [her] horizons" (30), but will she be in the middle forever, destined to be straddling two cultures?

In the final part of "A Wife's Story" Panna has to face up to the question of which way she would have to finally lean when her husband comes to New York to spend his holiday with her. She realizes then that the relationship between them has changed in a way that she secretly approves and he never will accept. For example, it occurs to her now that she does not know if she is unhappy to be doing the "man's jobs" in New York, such as making all the travel arrangements, which makes him a dependent. Her husband is not out of sorts in America; he delights in the sights and sounds of New York and the country's consumer culture as would any tourist from an underdeveloped country, and he enjoys having something of a second honeymoon with her. But while his thoughts are always about going back, she is continually reminded when with him that she has been slowly adjusting herself to America. A man from Yugoslavia that she meets on a sightseeing trip to the Statue of Liberty with her husband makes her think "whole peoples have moved before me; they've adapted" (*Middleman,* 39). Not surprisingly, then, when near the end of his vacation her husband suddenly asks her to abandon her studies and return to India with him, she has a feeling of dread. She is, after all, not an innocent abroad, nor does she want to quit her studies or the life she has in New York now. The story concludes with Panna standing naked before a mirror getting ready to make love to her husband the night before he will fly back to India, but by this time she has an answer to the question that has been in the back of her mind all the time. She will make love to him that night, but the woman watching the mirror she realizes is "free, afloat, watching somebody else" (*Middleman,* 41). She has, in effect, decided to veer away from the middle and become her own self, a single woman in America, although she will play at being a wife for another day.

If Panna Bhatt, already far away from home, is about to break loose, Maya Sanyal, the central character of "The Tenant" and the third of the three stories in *The Middleman* about married Indian women in America, is already a free woman, at least in the sense that she is no longer married and is able to do whatever she likes with her life. With a Ph.D. in comparative literature, a teaching job at the University of North Iowa, American citizenship, experience of life in New Jersey and North Carolina, a failed marriage to a white American, and a history of promiscuous relationships with numerous white Americans behind her, Maya should feel liberated from her Indian past. Yet she, too, is in a bit of a muddle about her affiliations. She has thus been on the lookout for "exotic spice stores" in Cedar Falls and in the neighboring city of Waterloo and has scoured the area's phone directory to find out if she can strike up "culinary intimacies" with Indians (*Middleman,* 97). Moreover, although she has slept with all kinds of men in America, she still seems to hunger for an affair with an Indian man.

Almost inevitably, Maya gets a chance to taste Indian food again as well as meet an Indian man in Cedar Falls. Dr. Chaterji, a Bengali like her and also on the faculty of the University of North Iowa, invites her for tea with his family. The evening passes smoothly, and she finds herself in a "deliquescent mood" (*Middleman,* 103). Nevertheless, she does not like Dr. Chaterji's pomposity or distaste for America and Americans. When Dr. Chaterji makes a pathetic attempt to seduce her later that night, she has no problems in shaming him in her best well-brought-up manner. But far from getting a distaste for Indian men from this episode, the next day she initiates a date in an airport transit lounge with Ashoke Mehta, an Indian physician working in Hartford, Connecticut, whose name she has picked up from going through the personals column of the *India Abroads* [*sic*] journal for "a suitable man" (*Middleman,* 108). When they meet, he appears to be emancipated enough for her. They seem to like each other and agree to meet again in the future.

Back from the date, Maya gives in to the desire building up within her by having an affair with her landlord, a man named Fred who has no arms but who proves to be a good companion and lover. When Ashoke Mehta rings her up again a few months later, however, she is ready to unhouse herself again and move out from Cedar Falls, abandon Fred, and join the Indian doctor in Hartford. Rootless, lonely—destined always to be a tenant—and driven by her sexuality, Maya is made by Mukherjee to be the type of the new Indian immigrant woman in North

America who is emotionally in transit but who yearns for a satisfactory relationship with a liberated Indian man. For all her promiscuity, then, Maya is still in the middle, caught between two worlds, located, as Elizabeth Ward puts it, in "exactly the no-man's-land inhabited by so many of Bharati Mukherjee's characters."[3] Mukherjee herself has described Maya as "a very lost, sad character, who really went out and married a white man and is so well attuned to women intellectuals, her colleagues, but at the same time there is that desire for a wholeness, nostalgia, that India and Indian traditions promised" (1990 interview, 20). Although Mukherjee does not say so explicitly, the ending of "The Tenant" indicates that Maya's relationship with Ashok Mehta may be Maya's gamble to achieve that sense of wholeness without going back to India.

Maya Sanyal's casual attitude toward sex is symptomatic of the moral license America seems to give to its immigrants. Indeed, Mukherjee writes a number of stories specifically to exhibit the violence, the lawlessness, and the licentiousness the new immigrants can get into and the illicit operations or shady dealings they can take part in. Alfie Judah, the protagonist of the titular story, is perhaps the best example of a middleman who does not bother about scruples and who thrives in turmoil and terror. When his narrative opens Alfie is in a Central American republic that is fighting off a revolution. Alfie is a "middleman" in this world, a hired gunman working for what appears to be a syndicate specializing in the arms trade. (This syndicate is managed by the country's corrupt president and an American businessman on the run from his country's legal system.) Tough, cynical, and well-traveled—he lists Baghdad, Bombay, and Queens as previous stops—Alfie appears unable to stay away from trouble. As he puts it, "My fresh [American] citizenship is always in jeopardy. My dealings can't stand too much investigation" (*Middleman*, 3). In the course of the narrative he makes love to a woman who was the president's mistress and is the businessman's wife as well as a guerrilla commander and witnesses the guerrillas executing the businessman. Alfie survives this round of violence—as he probably did many such rounds before—and at the end of the story is seen walking back to the capital of the republic, ready to trade in his knowledge of the guerrillas and their latest operation for cash. He seems destined, however, to return to America, even though "there are aspects of American life I came too late for and never will understand" (*Middleman*, 4).

Seen in the perspective of Mukherjee's literary career till this point, "The Middleman" is an unusual story for her to write, but as the first and titular story of the collection, it announces clearly her determination to venture as far away as possible from her milieu to write about all sorts of people caught up in a global diaspora. Jonathan Raban has characterized Mukherjee's fictional version of that diaspora as "a haphazard, pepperpot dispersal" and her characters as "chronic travelers who live, as travelers do, from minute to minute, dangerously free of both past and future."[4] Mukherjee has explained that she came to write the story of Alfie Judah "because he was a cynical person and a hustler, as many immigrant survivors have to be" (1988 interview, 648). Clearly, Mukherjee has now entered a phase in her work where she is bent on hazarding all her resources as a writer to bring into her fiction even the most hard-boiled immigrant and represent his "hustlerish kind of energy" (1988 interview, 654), but "The Middleman" proves that she is capable of pulling off such a trick.

"Danny's Girls" also takes us to the shadowy world of some of the new immigrants. This time the setting is a Flushings ghetto where immigrant entrepreneurs like Danny thrive by perfecting one scam after another. Although barely out of his teens, Danny has already acquired whatever is needed to become "a merchant of opportunity" (*Middleman*, 136), graduating from bets and scalping tickets in concerts organized for the immigrant Indian community to fixing beauty contests to becoming a pimp masquerading as a marriage broker. "Importing" attractive young South Asian "brides" for older, unattractive men, or baiting Indian men who would pay a good amount to "proxy-marry" American girls of Indian origin to get U.S. citizenship (*Middleman*, 137), Danny has become the consummate hustler, acquiring in the process power and, at least in the eyes of some of his fellow immigrants, a kind of mystique.

"Danny's Girls," however, is not so much about Danny Sahib as it is about its unnamed 15-year-old narrator. An admirer of Danny's schemes, and in Danny's pay despite his age, the narrator is the son of Indian immigrants who have come to the United States after being denied citizenship, first by Idi Amin, and then by an act of the British parliament. Although America has provided a home to them courtesy of the narrator's Aunt Lini, another ghetto entrepreneur (she is into loan-sharking), the family has fallen on hard times in the country. His father, in fact, has abandoned them, and his mother now sells papers in subway kiosks, dreaming the immigrant dream of sending her son to engineer-ing school at Columbia. Growing up in the ghettos, the narrator, how-ever, has no illusions about the route to be taken to fulfill the American dream. He helps Danny acquire "bride volunteers" for a sum, or distrib-utes posters of his girls as his agent. But he knows that the best option available to him in becoming someone important is to have a job that would give him "a freedom like Danny's but without the scams" (*Middleman,* 140). Level-headed in these matters, he knows that the most he can hope for is a SAT score that will allow him at least to go to Pace or Adelphi's engineering school.

Nevertheless, the narrator is also infatuated with one of Danny's "imports," a beautiful Nepalese who calls herself Rosie. He is jealous about her "gentlemen callers" (*Middleman,* 141) and somewhat confused about his feelings for a girl that he is attracted to but knows he will not be marrying. When in the climax of the story, however, Danny taunts him for his devotion to Rosie, he rebels against him, dumps his posters of his girls, and grabs hold of a very drunk Rosie. His act of defiance and possession of one of Danny's girls signals his entry into manhood; as he sees it, "For the first time I felt my life was going to be A-Okay" (*Middleman,* 145). "Danny's Girls" is thus in some ways a rites-of-pas-sage story; making love to Rosie is his way of resolving his problems and announcing that he has now come into his own in the tough and tawdry world of the immigrant.

Like the narrator of "Danny's Girls," the protagonist of "Jasmine" is an Indian teenager who will decisively come into her own in America through a sexual encounter. Like him, too, Jasmine is the product of an Indian diaspora that made their ancestors leave India and settle in far-away places. But while the narrator's parents came to the United States legally from Uganda, Jasmine has left her parents back in Trinidad and has come to Michigan as an illegal immigrant via Canada after negotiat-ing for herself a "smooth, bargain-priced emigration" (*Middleman,* 130) in Port of Spain. Jasmine has moved to the United States because she is ambitious and has come to realize that "Trinidad was an island stuck in the middle of nowhere" (*Middleman,* 124), a dead end for someone whose wits are about her.

Once in Michigan, Jasmine works first in a Detroit motel run by the Daboos, a family of Trinidadian Indians who also "ran a service fixing up illegals with islanders who had made it legally" (*Middleman,* 125). Like Danny Sahib or Aunt Lini, the Daboos are hustlers, involved in all types of schemes and even scams to supplement their income from the motel.

But because she knows she is working for the Daboos for exploitation pay, and because she feels impatient to do something with her life, she breaks away from the Daboos. Taking advantage of a dance party she goes to with the Daboo girls, a party arranged by the West Indian Students Association in the student union's building at Ann Arbor, she gets a job as a household helper with Bill and Lara Moffit. Bill is a professor of molecular biology, and Lara, she gathers, is a "performance artist" (*Middleman,* 128).

Working at a job similar to that of the family servant her parents engaged in Trinidad ought to be shameful for Jasmine, but she actually begins to enjoy her situation with the Moffits. She has a room of her own, a television, reasonable pay, the prospects of a college education before her, and friendly employers; she remembers Trinidad now only as a "shabby place" where "life was full of despair and drink and wanting" and Trinidadians as people who were "grasping and cheating and lying" (*Middleman,* 129). Indeed, by the time she meets the Daboos again to celebrate Christmas and New Year's Eve with them, she has started to think of them, too, as rustics working in an unpleasant environment.

One day when Lara is away on a tour with her performing group, Jasmine lets herself be seduced by Bill. The sexual encounter makes her feel good and gives her the sense of having arrived at a moment when she will be able to control her destiny decisively. She does not forget that she is still an illegal immigrant in America with nothing "other than what she wanted to invent and tell," but she cannot help feeling exhilarated, as did the narrator of "Danny's Girls" when he embraced Rosie, at launching off "wildly into the future" (*Middleman,* 135).

In a *Voice Literary Supplement* review of Mukherjee's short fiction, Polly Shulman has described "Jasmine" as a "particularly chilling" example of the writer's depiction of new immigrants "because the heroine has no idea she's being exploited" and because she is typical of Mukherjee characters who emerge from the ruins of tradition and rush pell-mell into "shame, disaster, and glorious riches."[5] Mukherjee, however, disagrees with reviewers such as Shulman, who have seen in Jasmine's embrace of Bill an example of the exploitation of a vulnerable young immigrant woman by her white male employer. She had wanted the scene to show that Jasmine is the one who is "in charge" in the encounter: "The man has succumbed to lust and to her sexuality," but "Jasmine is a woman who knows the power, is discovering the power of her sexuality" (1990 interview, 22). She meant the ending of the story to be "political" in the sense that Jasmine is displacing someone like Lara, "whose feminism and professionalism are built on the backs of underemployed Caribbean or Hispanic au-pair girls" (1990 interview, 22). Mukherjee said that she made Jasmine a Trinidadian because Trinidad was Naipaul's birthplace and she was using this fact to challenge "Naipaul's thesis of tragedy being geographical" (1990 interview, 26). Unlike Naipaul, the mentor who taught Mukherjee to depict "the aloofness of expatriation" in her earlier fiction, she has designed Jasmine's progress to show that you do not have to be "doomed to an incomplete and worthless little life" just because you are born in an island far from the center of the world (1990 interview, 27). Her riposte to Naipaul now that she is on to the "exuberance of immigration" is to tell him through someone like Jasmine, "Hey, look at Jasmine. She's smart, desirous, and ambitious enough to make something of her life" (1990 interview, 27).

Mr. Venkatesan, the protagonist of "Buried Lives," never manages to reach the American shore for which he heads after leaving his native Sri Lanka. His story parallels Jasmine's, however, in that it, too, ends satisfactorily for him in a sexual embrace after he has managed to come up to Hamburg through the underground route taken by Tamils from South Asia to land in North America. Mukherjee has said that she had originally planned to show Mr. Venkatesan being drowned when he and other refugees were being hurriedly unloaded onto a boat by an unscrupulous captain trying to evade the Coast Guard. But in writing his story, Mukherjee found out that "the guy wouldn't get on the boat. He found ways of hanging around, staying on in Germany. Then he found a girlfriend and she gave him necessary visa papers" (1990 interview, 29–30).

Mr. Venkatesan's resilience, of course, is the reason that his narrative belongs to *The Middleman* and not to the Canadian phase of Mukherjee's work. Mukherjee treats his quest to escape from his strife-torn island wryly, for he embarks on his voyage only after a series of misadventures and is a very unlikely candidate for any quest narrative. Indeed, when we first see him in the North Sri Lankan Tamil town of Trincomalee, this 49-year-old schoolteacher appears doomed to the kind of gray and hopeless life described in his favorite Matthew Arnold poem, "Buried Lives." Despite himself, however, he gets entangled in his country's civil war and is forced to contemplate the life of an exile. At first, he tries legitimate ways of escape from Sri Lanka, such as applying for admission and financial assistance to American universities. He describes himself in the personal essay he has to write for his applications as "a shadow-man, a nothing" in "this small dead-end island" (*Middleman,* 155), inspired to dream about going abroad, by the nineteenth-century adventures of G. A. Henty and A. E. W. Mason who, it is interesting to note, made many an Englishman imagine a colonial career through their fictions. When all his applications are rejected, he settles for some time in another dream world, where he can see himself "safely on America's heartland, with his own wife and car and all accoutrements of New World hearth and home" (*Middleman,* 156–57). Eventually, he gets in touch with a middleman who will arrange illegal emigration to Canada for a price.

And so Mr. Venkatesan embarks on his quest, reversing the direction taken by his favorite Henty and Mason heroes in their stories. In another neat piece of irony—diaspora narratives, Mukherjee implies, are full of such route reversals and ironies—his first stop is Tuticorin, India, the town that his ancestors "had left to find their fortunes in Ceylon's tea-covered northern hills" (*Middleman,* 160). From Tuticorin, he takes a train to Delhi, from Delhi an Aeroflot plane flies him to (East) Berlin via Moscow, and from this point he is smuggled across the border in a truck by an Algerian. Next, he is driven to Hamburg in a BMW by a Ghanian-born Berliner. Mr. Venkatesan's education in the phenomenon of diasporic populations continues when a Surinam-born German Tamil immigration lawyer takes him on as a case to stay deportation orders. This lawyer then deposits him with his cousin, a widow who runs a boarding house for people like Mr. Venkatesan, who appear destined forever to be in transit. Here, however, Mr. Venkatesan's fantastic-seeming but no doubt probable story ends as he finds romance and the promise of a German citizenship because of the widow.

Mukherjee's point in these stories is to focus our attention on the energies or potential unleashed even in people as timid as Mr. Venkatesan by their diasporic experience. All too conscious of the complex and ambivalent emotions generated in the voyagers to the New World, she uses many of the stories of *The Middleman* to highlight the fluid morality America's newest citizens almost inevitably exhibit as they struggle to root themselves in the continent. But Mukherjee is also aware that as they adapt to America in any way they can, older Americans will react variously, too, to their untraditional neighbors, colleagues, or acquaintances from Asia. A few of them, of course, will react bitterly or noncommittally to the transformations taking place in their country because of the new arrivals, but others will be reminded by the newcomers of America's essential "restlessness and fluidity"[6] and will come to accept them as an inescapable and even desirable part of their society.

Jeb Marshall, the emotionally scarred Vietnam veteran of "Loose Ends" is one of those Americans who will refuse to accept the changes wrought in their country by Asians (and Latinos). His life has gone downhill since Vietnam, and he feels bitter and disillusioned. As his wife observes, he is "at loose ends" (*Middleman*, 43). He is rankled by, among other things, the news that his wife will not be given a job by a Sikh employer. Full of righteous indignation, he asks rhetorically, "Who let these guys in?" He cannot get over what he has seen in the parking lot of a local mall: a blond swami levitating on a flying mat, a symbol of Americans taking off on an alien culture. From his jaundiced perspective, people like him and his wife have become "coolie labor in our own country" (*Middleman*, 44). His glory days were when he was on mission in Vietnam, but now he is only a hitman for a Mafioso type, his marriage has gone stale, and violent veterans like him are getting harsh sentences from unsympathetic judges. He has survived Vietnam, but America does not seem to care. "Where did America go?" he cannot help wondering (*Middleman*, 47). As far as he is concerned, while he and his fellow soldiers were "barricading the front door," someone "left the back door open" for all kinds of undesirable people and aliens (*Middleman*, 48). He used to love the Florida that "was built for your pappy and grammie" but feels that the state is now being run by locusts and sharks from Havana or Beirut, middlemen who ply their wares and fight deadly wars in their new tropical battlefield (*Middleman*, 50).

In the course of his narrative Jeb's wife leaves him, he kills a hoodlum who has been a threat to his boss, and he is instructed to lie low for a while. His way of doing so is to hijack a car, but in no time at all he is himself robbed of most of his "pay" for his assignment and thrown out of the car by two hijackers. Forced to walk to the nearest motel on a highway just outside of Miami, he is in a vicious mood when he walks up to the service counter an hour before midnight. He storms into the staff area, only to find it full of "brown people sitting cross-legged on the floor of a regular motel room and eating with their hands" (*Middleman*, 52). But what really infuriates him is the way they look at him: "A bunch of aliens and they stare like I'm the freak" (*Middleman*, 52). When one of them jokes that what they were really running was a " 'po-tel' because he is 'A Patel owning a motel'" (*Middleman*, 53), Jeb is even more irritated.

Though Jeb is at a boiling point, the group appears not to notice his anger. The knowledge that he is a nobody to them touches him at a point where he is already sore: "While we were nailing up that big front door, these guys were sneaking in around back. They got their money, their family networks, and their secretive languages" (*Middleman,* 53). The last straw for him is the look of "distaste for the likes of me" (*Middleman,* 55) he gets from the Patel girl who shows him to his room when he refuses to pay an advance on it. All the frustration, rage, and resentment building up within him make him go berserk, and he rapes and then kills her, thinking with his twisted logic that in doing violence to her he was getting back at everything that was "taking" America away from people like him. It is a violent climax to a powerful story written to demonstrate that in the United States of the 1980s there was no way one could ignore the new Americans from Asia and to emphasize that only the already maladjusted older Americans can try to alter this fact.

The problem with Griff, the "low-level money manager" (*Middleman,* 78) protagonist of "Fighting for the Rebound," is not that he rejects the new Americans but that he has become too jaded to understand the depth of their commitment to belong. He cannot, therefore, understand the intensity of his current girlfriend, Blanquita. For him, this beautiful woman is just another of his conquests, someone with whom he can have a brief affair. That she is a Filipino matters to him only in the sense that it is something to have a relationship with someone exotic. What he cannot perceive is that Blanquita is desperately attempting to enter a relationship that will offer her stability and security. Because her family has come down in the world with the fall of the Marcos regime—her father was a Marcos crony who now works in a liquor store in California—she "likes to act as though real life began for her at JFK when she got past the customs and immigration on the seventeenth of October, 1980" (*Middleman,* 79). Her declaration of love for him strikes him as "tragically sincere" (*Middleman,* 80), but he has a sense of déjà vu and is just too cynical about such overt display of sentiments. Moreover, while he might have a taste for things exotic, he finds "real foreign . . . a little scary" (*Middleman,* 81).

But if Griff is too superficial, too self-centered, and too suspicious of genuine emotions to commit himself to a lasting relationship with Blanquita, he is also aware that none of his other conquests made him feel "this special, this loved" (*Middleman,* 82). And so when Blanquita, in a desperate bid to have Griff reveal the depth of his feelings for her, tells him that she has been invited out by her chief, he cannot help saying, "I don't want you to go." In saying even this much he thinks he is not being himself and is apprehensive of being seen as "a romantic in red suspenders" (*Middleman,* 82). He decides, therefore, not to give up anymore of himself for her sake. Frustrated, she accuses him and his culture of narcissism and of not knowing how to love: "You're all emotional cripples. All you Americans. You just worry about your own measly little relationships. You don't care how much you hurt the world" (*Middleman,* 83).

Griff does manage to calm Blanquita down on this occasion by taking charge as he thinks only Americans can. "It's okay for a nation of pioneers to bully the rest of the world as long as the cause is just" is how he explains his imperial strategy in handling what he cynically labels Blanquita's "Green Card politics" to make him commit himself to her by holding out the chief as a rival (*Middleman,* 84). But Griff overestimates his ability to placate Blanquita and underestimates the intensity of her desire to go for a permanent relationship. She leaves him for the chief as she threatened to do, and he gets back to his yuppie life-style: jogging, watching a lot of TV, and one more casual relationship of the type he always got into before he met Blanquita. He has a nagging feeling this time, however, that he is just going through the motions and feels a little tired of the routine he had followed so glibly till now. Nevertheless, when in the conclusion of the story Blanquita phones to tell him she has left the chief because he, too, will not commit himself to her and pleads for him to come and pick her up, what catches his attention is the line his newest girlfriend delivers as she leaves him. Deciding that a call from his ex-lover is her cue for abandoning him, the girlfriend declares, "I don't want to start anything complicated" (*Middleman,* 94). The line could be his motto, too, for Griff has resisted Blanquita precisely for this reason. But Mukherjee concludes the story in such a way that we cannot be sure that he will not go beyond this noncommittal perspective on life and respond to Blanquita's cry for love.

The conclusion of "Fathering" leaves readers with no doubt, however, that Jason, its narrator-protagonist, will decide to respond positively to the demands made on his emotions by his half-Vietnamese daughter, Eng. Jason fathered Eng when he had a fling with a Vietnamese barmaid while serving with the army in Saigon. Eng spent her early years in Vietnam and seems to have been traumatized by the war, the loss of her mother, and the dislocation in her life that has brought her to Rock Springs (a small town Mukherjee has located in upstate New York). She has been brought over to America partly because Jason wanted her to be with him and partly because his common-law wife, Sharon, thought that he should come to terms with his past. But having this strange and sickly child has strained Jason's relationship with Sharon. In fact, Sharon now views Eng as a threat, while Eng wants to monopolize her father. Jason sees in Eng "a sick, frightened, foreign kid" (*Middleman,* 116), as well as his daughter, but Sharon thinks that the child is either being manipulative or has become mentally unhinged. She tells him that the child needs a doctor and not him.

As the story begins, Jason decides to ignore Sharon's diagnosis and puts the bruised Eng—she seems to have a fever but has also apparently been pressing coins into her flesh to mutilate herself—to sleep. Depressed and hurt by what she thinks is Jason's indifference to her and excessive concern for Eng, Sharon leaves the house in a huff to consult the family physician, Dr. Kearns. As he watches over the sleeping child, Jason hears Eng having nightmares where she relives the brutality of American soldiers who shot her grandmother. He cannot help wondering then if his daughter's "Asian skin bruises differently from ours" (*Middleman,* 118). But if he thinks that she is essentially different from him, he also wants to be a good father to her. He thus tries to read to her to calm her down. Ironically, the book he reads to her is a science fiction novel about aliens who have "taken over small towns all over the country . . . no state is safe from aliens" (*Middleman,* 119). This, indeed, could be the theme of *The Middleman* as a whole; Mukherjee is bent on using its stories to drive home the point that the United States is now being flooded by immigrants who have been traditionally perceived as aliens and who must now be acknowledged and accepted by older Americans.

In "Fathering" Jason thus represents liberal America. He is, after all, totally unlike Jeb Marshall, the xenophobic Vietnam veteran of "Loose Ends," in that he is dedicated to the idea that America should acknowledge the consequences of its relationship to Asia. Should America continue to see its newer citizens as aliens, or should it embrace them without reservations and take them along to whatever future it has? In Jason's narrative the question is posed to him when Dr. Kearns asks him to come over with Eng so that he can examine the child and talk to him about the distraught Sharon. In an emotionally high-pitched scene in Dr. Kearns's chamber, Sharon urges Jason, in effect, to choose between Eng and herself. His daughter, on the other hand, tells him, wildly, to send Sharon away. Driven to choose between them, Jason realizes that he feels guilty about what he has done and will do to Sharon but that the imperative for him at this point of his life is his "alien child" (*Middleman,*

121). As the story ends, then, Jason has arrived at a decision; he will take Eng away and plunge into the future with her "in the cold chariot" of his van (*Middleman,* 122).

Renata de Marcos, the narrator of "Orbiting," has no problems with having an affair and giving herself up wholly to her Asian-American boyfriend, Roshan. An upper-class refugee from the civil war in Afghanistan, Roshan works in a restaurant in New York and plans to eventually earn a degree in electrical engineering. Despite being cosmopolitan and well-bred, he has a foreignness of manners and a sensibility that Renata finds irresistible. "Orbiting" is therefore not a story where the narrator-protagonist has to come to terms with her feelings for an alien. Instead, the problem Mukherjee poses is whether the rest of Renata's family will accept Roshan as one of their own. Older Americans themselves, will they take to her Afghan boyfriend? Renata's father, we gather, is a second-generation American of Italian origin, her mother a Spanish woman her father met on a European holiday. Her sister Cindy is married to an Amish American named Brent. All of them, however, have been more or less transformed by America and have come to accept its values and its culture. Will they approve of someone as unassimilated as Roshan is?

Renata is afraid, then, that in having become completely Americanized, her family will not remember their own immigrant past and will find Roshan too exotic for their tastes. Consequently, she is quite tense about the outcome of the Thanksgiving dinner where her family will get the opportunity to meet Roshan for the first time. "All over the country," she reassures herself before the dinner, "women are towing new lovers home to meet their families" (*Middleman,* 63). But while the fact that he is totally unlike any man she has ever known is the reason she feels so attracted to him, she cannot help reflecting as she introduces him to her family that "my parents are so parochial" (*Middleman,* 69).

As the Thanksgiving Day dinner encounter begins, all her worst fears about the dinner turning into a disaster seem to be coming true. Her father, for example, thinks Afghanistan is somewhere in Africa and starts calling Roshan Roy. Roshan, for his part, says something about the odorlessness of American flowers, which she knows her mother will find offensive. He then makes her father's face go livid by declining to drink whiskey with him because drinking is a taboo in his religion. Franny, Brent's petulant teenage daughter from a previous marriage, starts smirking at Roshan's obvious foreignness. Brent tries to help by getting Roshan involved in a conversation about professional basketball, but Roshan admits he knows nothing about the game. Renata knows that Roshan "is so sophisticated, he could make monkeys" out of them all, and yet she is afraid her family was beginning to see him as "a retard" (*Middleman,* 73).

At the end, though, the Thanksgiving Day dinner turns out to be a success, and Roshan proves to be quite a hit with Renata's family. What finally endears him to them is his passionate exposition of the situation in Afghanistan and the circumstances that led him to flee his country. It is something of a "revelation" for Brent, for instance, that "a reasonably educated and rational man like Ro would die for things that he . . . has never heard of and would rather laugh about" (*Middleman,* 74). Renata's father is stunned by the intricacies of the route Roshan took to come to America and begins to appreciate the meaning of Thanksgiving more clearly than he has ever done before. Roshan impresses also with his carving skills; he does such a good job on the turkey that he has even Franny "practically licking his fingers" (*Middleman,* 75). As for Renata, her feeling for Roshan has now been transformed into hero worship. In fact, as the story ends, she comes to see Roshan as the archetypal American hero, "Clint Eastwood, scarred hero and survivor," a man beside whom her father and brother-in-law are children (*Middleman,* 76). She realizes, of course, that there are things American that Roshan has still to learn, but she knows that these are relatively simpler than what he has already experienced. Ro is her chance, she is convinced, "to heal the world" (*Middleman,* 76).

"Orbiting" is without a doubt the most optimistic of the stories of *The Middleman.* Liew-Geok Leong's comment on the story is very apt: "In the movement from immigrant subcultures to mainstream culture that *The Middleman* represents, 'Orbiting' is striking for the very Americanizing process it celebrates" (Leong, 498). It is a story Mukherjee appears to have deliberately written as her Thanksgiving offering for the melting-pot process of American culture that was allowing immigrants from Asia to successfully root themselves in the New World and to transform it as well as themselves. Certainly it substantiates Mukherjee's claim that what she wants to do through her fiction is more than tell a story or create a memorable character and that her ultimate intention is "to redefine the nature of *American* and what makes an American" ("Woman," 25).

The Middleman and Other Stories thus approaches from a variety of angles the striking changes occurring in American society and culture as well as in the American psyche by new and nontraditional immigrants to the country. Throughout the volume Mukherjee keeps directing the reader's gaze at the interpenetration of America by Asians. Seen as a whole, the stories point to an American landscape that is starting to be dotted with Asian ghettos and businesses. The Indian settlement of Flushings, Queens; the Brooklyn neighborhood that Roshan has dubbed "Little Kabul"; names such as Patel or Abdul; and "the aisles of bok choy and twenty kinds of Jamaican spices" at the Atlanta Farmers' Market are some of the instances inserted by Mukherjee to remind her readers that "the US of A is still a pioneer country" ("Fighting for the Rebound," *Middleman,* 79). The pages of *The Middleman* are full of people such as Mr. Venkatesan of "Buried Lives" who wish "to flee abroad and seize the good life as had his San Jose cousin" (159), of new Americans dreaming the American dream and realizing or half-realizing that dream in startling ways. Mukherjee also fictionalizes the way people shed parts of themselves and acquire new identities in America, the way in which the American melting pot makes in no time a Ro or a Roy out of a Roshan. Jonathan Raban is therefore right to say in his review of *The Middleman* that, taken together, the volume represents "a romance with America itself, its infinitely possible geography, its license, sexiness and violence" (Raban, 22).

One other point Raban makes about *The Middleman* is that it is a distinctive collection at least partly because of the dexterity with which Mukherjee uses the monologue form in most of the stories and the "rapturous affection and acuteness of ear" Mukherjee displays in capturing "the idiom of America in the 1980s." This aspect of Mukherjee's accomplishment reminds Raban of the success of Nabokov, another immigrant writer whose 1950 novel *Lolita* exhibited his ability to capture the idiom of contemporary America. Seeing it from the perspective of its use of American speech, Raban calls *The Middleman,* too, "a consummated romance with the American language" (Raban, 22).

Mukherjee has claimed that from *Darkness* onward she had "begun appropriating the American language" ("Woman," 26). But only in Shawn Patel's narrative of his quest to find wholeness in a fragmented world in "Saints" has Mukherjee handled the monologue form with anything like the adroitness she displays in representing American speech in almost all the stories of *The Middleman.* In "A Wife's Story" Panna Bhatt comments on the way her diction has changed in the time she has spent in America. Bhatt's comments on this change reveals something of the attention that Mukherjee pays to the nuances of the spoken language in situating a character: "That part of my life is over, the way *trucks* have replaced *lorries* in my vocabulary" (*Middleman*, 31). But Panna can also sound poetic as she depicts the sun breaking through over New York City: "The summer sun pushes through fluffy clouds and dapples the glass of office towers" (*Middleman*, 37).

Both Jeb Marshall's Vietnam experience and the atmosphere of menace that surrounds him come out clearly in his one-sentence account of his success in killing his boss's rival: "I did what I was paid for; I eliminated the primary target and left no traces" (*Middleman*, 47). Griff's fondness for stock-market jargon, for sports metaphors, and for the appurtenances of yuppie life are everywhere in evidence in his narrative in "Fighting for the Rebound." Sometimes Mukherjee experiments with mixing registers and in showing her characters moving between languages. Gita Rajan thus points out the way Mukherjee shows Eng shuttling "between perfectly normal, American use of the English language and curses/war slang in Vietnamese" in "Fathering" to reveal "her position between two cultures and her splintered psyche" (Rajan, 239). While Mukherjee's ability to reproduce the American vernacular and to introduce the idioms of new immigrants is impressive in *The Middleman*, her ear for Indian English seems to have deteriorated considerably in the volume; when someone such as Dr. Chaterji speaks in "The Tenant" he almost becomes a parody of Indians speaking English.

On the whole, though, *The Middleman and Other Stories* shows a confident Mukherjee working dexterously on her theme of the making of new Americans and ringing all kinds of fascinating variations on that theme. Reviewers were almost unanimous in their praise of Mukherjee's handling of her subject matter and her skillful use of the American language. It is no wonder that the volume garnered for Mukherjee her only major laurel to date, the National Book Critics Circle Award for Fiction, and that it was a commercial as well as a critical success. Indeed, it is not too much to say that with the publication of *The Middleman* Mukherjee had registered her claim to be considered one of the leading authors of contemporary America. The widespread acclaim for the book would be eventually followed by one or two tough-minded critiques of it (see Knippling, 143–61), but from now on Mukherjee's presence in American letters could no longer be ignored.

Jasmine

Mukherjee has said that she did not initially plan on expanding "Jasmine"—the short story in *The Middleman* about the exuberant Trinidadian girl who becomes an illegal immigrant relishing America—into a novel. But the story's resilient and adventurous heroine was a character Mukherjee "fell in love with," since she was the type of person her creator "would have liked to have been" (1990 interview, 18). Mukherjee said that she continued to think about Jasmine until the clear-sighted Trinidadian teenager became in her consciousness "a deeper, more complicated character" (1990 interview, 19). As Mukherjee reflected on further developing the story's plot so that it could make for a more compelling work about inventing and re-inventing a self through immigration in America, she concluded that she had to re-create the setting and complicate Jasmine and her situation in other ways. Instead of the limited but relatively fluid world of Trinidad, Mukherjee felt that she would have to give the heroine of the new work "a society that was so repressive, traditional, so caste-bound, genderist, that she could discard it" more easily (1990 interview, 19). Mukherjee therefore set about to "find the metaphors and symbolic location" for her new reincarnation of Jasmine and began to devise "the right series of events" to dramatize the journey of a woman getting more into America and further away from her roots.

The narrator-heroine of *Jasmine* (1989), Mukherjee's third novel, is a woman from a village called Hasnapur in Punjab, a state in the northwestern corner of India. The novel depicts her growing up in a semi-feudal, rural, and patriarchal society until she marries Prakash Vijh, a progressive-minded and bright young man who gets admitted to a Florida institution that purportedly offers degrees in electronics. When Prakash is killed by a Sikh terrorist bomb, Jasmine decides to use all the money she is left with to travel to the Florida International Institute of Technology to commit *sati,* a Hindu ritual where a widow immolates herself for her husband's sake. Soon after she lands in Florida, however, she is raped by the sea captain who has smuggled her and other illegal immigrants to America. She manages to murder him and, considering herself defiled, abandons her plans to immolate herself. She is rescued by the kindly Lillian Gordon, who helps her travel to Flushing, New York, so that she can find a home with Prakash's mentor, Professor Devinder Vadhera, and his family. But she finds the life lived by Indians in this Queens ghetto constricting and opts to work as an au pair for Taylor

Hayes, a Columbia physicist, and Wylie Hayes, an editor in a publishing firm, and their adopted daughter, Duff. In the two years Jasmine is with them, the Hayeses separate, and Taylor falls in love with her. Still, when she sees the Sikh terrorist responsible for the death of Prakash in Central Park, she flees to Baden, Iowa, where she has an affair with Bud Ripplemeyer, a local banker. A shot fired by a client who has gone berserk paralyzes Bud, and out of sympathy for him she decides to have his child as well as adopt a teenage Vietnamese refugee called Du Thien with him. She finds the demands Bud makes on her a strain, however. When, at the end of her story, Taylor and Duff show up and Taylor asks her to join them as they resettle in California, a pregnant Jasmine agrees to go with them.

In expanding on the story's idea, then, Mukherjee makes ample use of the space afforded her by the novel form. Trinidad and Michigan are replaced by Punjab, Florida, New York, and Iowa; the limited third-person perspective used in the story gives way to first-person narration, and Jasmine becomes more of a sensitive survivor undergoing complex internal transformations than the shallow teenager who lives purely for the moment. But as the summary of *Jasmine* indicates, the basic plot situation of the novel follows that of the story: the Jasmine of the novel (as well as of the story) comes to America as an illegal immigrant, works as an au pair for an academic couple, and finds herself attracted to the professor husband who makes a move on her. Indeed, in some crucial ways the Jasmine of the novel who at its conclusion describes herself as someone "greedy with want and reckless from hope"[7] is not really that different from the Jasmine of the story.

Published only a year after *The Middleman*, *Jasmine* has links with other stories of the collection, too. The underground route taken by Jasmine to go to America from India parallels to some extent that taken by Mr. Venkatesan in "Buried Lives"; the Florida that is witness to much violence but which is being taken over by developers in "Loose Ends" is not unlike the Florida that we see in the novel; the Indian ghetto of Flushing that is Jasmine's home for five months is also the world in which the narrator of "Danny's Girls" grows up; everywhere in the novel, as in the collection of stories, are signs of an America undergoing massive demographic changes because of a flood of untraditional immigrants from Asia and South America. Just as we see Roshan in "Orbiting" becoming "Ro" for his white American lover, Renata, and "Roy" for her father, we see the inevitable Americanization induced by a melting-pot culture signified by the many names given to Jasmine by her American acquaintances. In fact, at least one passage from "Orbiting" where Roshan describes his experience as a transit passenger in international air travel—"I know too well the transit lounges of many airports. We travel the world with gym bags and prayer rugs, unrolling them in the transit lounges" (*Middleman*, 74)—has its distinct echo in Jasmine's description of the path taken by illegal immigrants like herself: "You see us sleeping in airport lounges; you watch us unwrapping the last of our native foods, unrolling our prayer rugs, reading our holy books" (*Jasmine*, 100).

But if *Jasmine* is affiliated to the short stories of *The Middleman*, it is not thematically unrelated to Mukherjee's two previous novels. As Ralph J. Crane has pointed out, while the female protagonists of her first two novels are identified in their titles by their relationship to their fathers or their husbands—a clear indication of "the restrictions imposed" on them culturally because of their gender—the heroine of this third novel has gradually refused to accept "invisibility" and ultimately rejects "imperial shackles."[8] Crane also sees another line of progression in the way in which Mukherjee increases the distances between herself and her protagonists from novel to novel. While Tara seems to be quite close to her, Dimple represents Indian wives in North America, and Jasmine exemplifies all immigrant women who have taken their destiny in their hands.

Crane approaches the novel as a female bildungsroman—that is, "as a novel which specifically traces the development of a female protagonist through various experiences and crises, into maturity, and more importantly, her self-identity and place in the world" (Crane 1992). Unlike Crane, who has only good things to say about the book, Gurleen Grewal offers a trenchant critique of it in her essay "Born Again American: The Immigrant Consciousness in *Jasmine*." But even Grewal sees in the novel an immigrant bildungsroman in that "it posits a norm of self-development."[9] As Grewal indicates through her sarcastic title, that development is oriented toward making Jasmine into someone embodying the spirit of America. Mukherjee clearly marks out six stages in Jasmine's character formation by the names she is given or not given by others: the name she gets at birth is Jyoti, her husband had called her Jasmine, Lillian Gordon's appellation for her is Jazzy, the Vadheras seem to have no name for her at all, Taylor calls her Jase, and Bud renames her as Jane. It is these stages in her growth that we will now follow.

Looking back at her life as Jyoti Vijh, the 24-year-old narrator Jasmine in her Jane Ripplemeyer reincarnation reveals that even as a child she had a mind of her own. In the first scene of the novel we observe the seven-year-old Jyoti rejecting what the village astrologer sees in her stars—widowhood and exile—and wounding herself in a gesture of defiance. The astrologer emphasizes to her that there was no changing fate, but Jasmine, already conscious of her female identity and armed with the belief that "she-ghosts" were guarding her, refuses to accept that she was "nothing" (*Jasmine*, 4). Jyoti also comes to realize early in her life that she was a survivor, "a fighter and adapter" (*Jasmine*, 40), because she knows that her mother's desperate bid to strangle her as an infant failed. It is not that her mother did not want a life for her; rather, she was afraid that as the fifth daughter of their impoverished family, Jyoti was destined to be a dowryless bride and she therefore wanted to spare her the ignominy (later, when Jasmine wants to pursue a higher education, it is her mother who convinces her father that a girl should have more than a primary education). Two other discoveries that Jyoti makes early in her life contribute to her feeling that she could cheat fate: she becomes conscious of her beauty and knows that she has a gift for picking up foreign languages.

Jasmine is especially proficient in English and devotes herself to the reading of novels written in that language. Four books she tries to read at that time but is forced to abandon because they prove to be too diffi-cult for a seven-year-old are *Shane, Alice in Wonderland, Great Expectations*, and *Jane Eyre. Shane*, of course, is the archetypal "frontier" narrative, and Jasmine probably unwittingly acquires from it her instinct to continually move westward; in America she is in a kind of glitzy wonderland and finds herself encountering strange situations and unusual characters as Alice did; the story of her education and character formation reminds us of the classic English bildungsroman by Dickens; and in the last phase of her adventures Jasmine is like Charlotte Brontë's heroine, a ministering Jane to a crippled and much older man who is totally dependent on her.

Even as a child, Jasmine shows herself to be someone who will not let the past rule her life. Although she has the refined and delicate features of her father and has his kind of presence around her, she cannot help think-ing that he was a fool to drown himself in nostalgia for Lahore, the city he had been forced to leave behind during the partition of India in 1947. She also seems to enjoy having a sense of power; when their rich neighbors get electricity, her favorite game is to put their light switch on and off for "with my palm in the light switch, I felt totally in control" (*Jasmine*, 44). Living as she does in a society that circumscribed women through all sorts of rules, she learns early to make use of every opportunity that came her way and all about "permissible rebellion" (*Jasmine*, 47).

Jasmine is also courageous and resourceful; when attacked by a mad dog in the Hasnapur fields, she is able to kill it with a staff she carries around with her because it makes her feel "the buzz of power" (*Jasmine*, 54). Her grandmother, disturbed that the teenage Jyoti wants to study and not marry, tells her, "Individual effort counts for nothing" (*Jasmine*, 57), but Jyoti will not be coaxed into abandoning her dreams of getting a better life through education. If the astrologer and her grandmother represent the fatalistic aspect of Hindu philosophy, the young Jyoti has an instinctive understanding of another belief enshrined in Hindu belief: "to treat every second of your existence as a possible assignment from God" (*Jasmine*, 61). Believing, then, that her mission was to somehow rise above her surroundings, Jasmine rejects despair and cynicism and believes that "she can move on and make a life for herself" (1990 interview, 25) because that was what God meant her to do.

So Jyoti continues her education, picking up knowledge not only from books but also from hearing men talk about politics, from newspapers and the radio, and from her brother's friend Prakash, who she is determined to marry even before she has met him because of his reputation for intelligence and sensitivity, because he has applied for jobs overseas, and because he is fluent in English. It is important to Jyoti that the man she marries knows English, for to have English as a language was to have "more than you had been given at birth, it was to want the world" (*Jasmine*, 69). Deliberately, she entices Prakash into marrying her, carefully calculating the effects she wants to have on him on their first date.

One way she sets out to influence Prakash's feeling in that first meeting is by sticking a jasmine wreath in her hair. It is not surprising, then, that when they get married two weeks later he decides to rename her Jasmine because she appeared to him destined to "quicken the whole world" with her perfume (*Jasmine*, 77). Undoubtedly, the international association Prakash makes with the name is the reason that the narrator chooses it for the title of her narrative over all the other names she has in it. Prakash is set on taking her away from her village and separating her from her past. As the older narrator sees him, Prakash was like a Professor Higgins out to remake her in the light of his own obsessions about progressive behavior and female education and of "doing better, making something more of . . . life than fate intended" (*Jasmine*, 85). He makes no sexual demands on her and, in fact, refuses to make her pregnant at 15. Content to be with him and dream his dreams, she prepares herself for life in America as a student's wife and for cheating fate, secure in the belief that "if we could just get away from India, then all fates would be canceled. We'd start with new stars. We could say or be anything we wanted. We'd be on the other side of the earth, out of God's sight" (*Jasmine*, 83).

But while husband and wife dream their dream, Punjab is in ferment because of demands by a section of the Sikh population for an independent Sikh nation, and, on the eve of their departure for America, Prakash is killed by a terrorist bomb. One-half of the astrologer's prediction— widowhood—comes true, leaving Jasmine in a daze. She blames herself for his death because the Sikh terrorist has apparently targeted her out of his hatred for Hindu women, and prepares to commit *sati*. For the moment, at least, she has forgotten Prakash's admonition to "stop regressing into the feudal Jyoti" (*Jasmine*, 92) and loses sight of her goals for self-development, independence, and emigration to America. Nevertheless, Prakash's exhortation to her from beyond life not to join other widows in her village in a life consecrated to dead husbands and to aim for America at the very least makes her think of committing *sati* in the Florida campus of his dreams.

Carrying with her a sandalwood Ganpati, the Hindu god with "an elephant trunk to uproot anything" in her path (*Jasmine*, 102), and possessing a singlemindedness of purpose, Jasmine lands in Florida. Once she is raped by the captain of the ship, however, she snaps out of the state of shock and mindlessness she had been in ever since Prakash's death. She is reminded just before the rape of the positive aspect of Hindu belief inculcated in her by her mother, which taught her that "we are all put on this earth for a purpose. . . . All acts are connected. For every monster there is a hero. For every hero, a monster" (*Jasmine*, 114). Because she has been defiled by being raped, she realizes that *sati* is no longer a way out for her, and she decides to opt for rebirth, to avenge herself on the monster. As Mukherjee has explained it, she becomes in the process Kali, "the goddess of destruction," "a destroyer of evil so that the world can be renewed" (1990 interview, 21).

Jasmine is now ready for her next reincarnation as Jazzy and lets herself be refashioned by Lillian Gordon, whose mission in life, it seems, is to help undocumented aliens survive in America. The second of the astrologer's prediction—exile—comes true, and yet Lillian Gordon will be the first of many individuals Jasmine meets in America who will allow her to do something with her fate that is tantamount to cheating it. As the older narrator explains it, combining the Hindu belief in reincarnation (explained to her, amazingly, by Mary Webb, a University of Iowa professor who is part of a bimonthly group taking lessons from a Hindu

guru in Dalton, Iowa) with the image of a record player, "I do believe
that extraordinary events can jar the needle arm, jump tracks, rip across
reincarnations, and deposit a life into a groove that was not prepared to
receive it" (*Jasmine,* 127). What Lillian Gordon does is not only make
her learn to live in the present without being burdened by the past but
also to, literally, "walk and talk American" (*Jasmine,* 134). She also helps
Jasmine get back her self-confidence and pays for her trip to New York
so that she can live with Professor Vadhera.

The Jasmine who arrives in New York, then, feels free of bitterness
and is full of the hope she had when with Prakash. But the five months
she spends with the Vadheras prove stifling for her. Although Professor
Vadhera is a kind man and his wife appears to be happy to have her as a
full-time unpaid maid in the house, Jasmine has become an invisible,
nameless woman in the Flushing ghetto. She knows that she wants
something more from life than what the Vadheras had from a full day's
work: just enough money to live in a Little India in New York City. She
is determined to leave her past behind, to keep away from the Jyoti that
she was, but that is impossible in an "apartment of artificially maintained Indianness" (*Jasmine,* 145) where she had been admitted as
Prakash's wife. Depressed at being rendered invisible and living in
limbo, and full of *"wanting"* (*Jasmine,* 142), she confesses to Professor
Vadhera her unhappiness at not having a "green card, even a forged one"
(*Jasmine,* 148), which would grant her back the freedom to be herself
and give her a name she could use again in the outside world. As soon as
the professor manages to get her a forged green card, Jasmine flees from
the Vadhera apartment and takes one more plunge into America.

Jasmine gets a job with the Hayeses through Kate Gordon-Feldstein,
Lillian's photographer daughter who lives only an hour's drive from
Flushing but whose life-style seems to be miles and miles away from the
Vadheras. The "incidental clutter" of Kate's studio thrills Jasmine and
speaks to her "of possibility," for it tells her "that one could live like this
and not be struck down" (*Jasmine,* 160). America had allowed Kate, this
girl from "a swampy backwater," to accomplish so much; why should
Jasmine's life be any different? Even the sight of Sam, a marine iguana
Kate keeps as a pet, inspires Jasmine and tells her that she has been
reborn and that there is no going back to the tropical world she has left
behind.

But it is in the two years that Jasmine spends with the Hayeses that
she emerges as completely her own woman and begins living the
American dream. Jasmine wants to embody the spirit of America

because "what America offers her . . . is the hope that things will turn out all right" in the end despite momentary setbacks (1990 interview, 25). Taylor and Wylie continue the process of teaching Jasmine to "walk and talk American" that Lillian Gordon had begun, and Jasmine finds fulfillment in mothering Duff. Significantly, she *wants* to be American and laps up everything she comes across in the Hayeses' apartment or the world outside it. As she notes, the conversation of guests, television, the language she heard on the street "all became *my* language, which I learned like a child, from the first words up. The squatting fields of Hasnapur receded fast" (*Jasmine,* 174). Jase, the name Taylor gives her, or Jassy, as Wylie calls her, typifies the casual yet intimate ambience of the couple's apartment. Jasmine prefers Jase to Jassy, however, partly because she is attracted to Taylor's "careless confidence and graceful self-absorption" (*Jasmine,* 171), and partly because this name gives her the feeling that she was living for the first time for herself and seizing the day. Since the Hayeses treated her as a part of their family, she feels that she had "landed and was getting rooted" (*Jasmine,* 179). Even when the Hayeses separate and Jasmine is reminded of the essential fluidity of America, she is able to take the break-up of the family in stride, although she concedes that "the hardest lesson of all" she had to learn about America was that in this country "nothing lasts" (*Jasmine,* 181).

With Wylie out of the way, Jasmine becomes more intimate with Taylor. Her American education continues at a brisk pace despite Wylie's absence, since every day she "made discoveries about the city" (*Jasmine,* 184). Taylor also plays a key role in her formation as an American by teaching her about baseball or about such basic things as returning unsolicited mail. Jasmine emphasizes, however, that Taylor does not want her to change; she "changed because she wanted to," having learned from her time with the Vadheras that "to bunker oneself inside nostalgia, to sheath the heart in a bulletproof vest, was to be a coward" (*Jasmine,* 185). But almost as soon as Taylor makes his declaration of love to her in the park, her fate catches up with her again in the shape of the Sikh terrorist who had killed her husband and who has now become a hot dog vendor in New York. The sight of the murderer is a sharp reminder to her that God's plan for her was to be an exile; fate had decreed that she must unhouse herself again and move on. And so she heads for Baden County, Iowa, solely because this was where Duff had been born, and becomes the common-law wife of the prosperous but middle-aged banker, Bud Ripplemeyer.

Jasmine meets Bud through his mother, Ma Ripplemeyer, who, like Lillian Gordon, is a do-gooder, helping uprooted people restart their lives in new surroundings. Despite her help and Bud's instant attraction to an exotic woman for whom he is willing to leave Karin, his wife of many years, Jasmine finds adjusting to Iowa another trial. In some ways, Iowa is like the Punjab she had left behind—a land of farmers, a place where traditional ways are suddenly being threatened and a few disgruntled people are reacting to difficult conditions caused by a drought either by leaving the state or by sudden acts of violence. There is a lot of hate around. Not only is Bud shot by a bankrupt client, but Jasmine has to face racist taunts from drunks in a bar that make her wish, for once, that she had "known America before it got perverted" (*Jasmine,* 201). Although she is a "Lazarus"—always rebounding from death-in-life—it hurts to be labeled a "gold digger" by someone such as Karin, Bud's ex-wife (*Jasmine,* 201). Occasionally, she feels too out of place and hears the astrologer of her childhood jibe at her, "foolish and wicked girl, did I not tell you you'd end up among aliens" (*Jasmine,* 203).

The maiming of Bud leaves Jasmine insecure, and she has moments of guilt about not reacting quickly to save him from his assailant, just as she had felt guilty about the death of Prakash. When Karin, attempting to hurt her, compares her to a tornado that leaves a path of destruction behind it, she feels stung. Having Du—the Vietnamese teenager Bud has adopted to atone for deserting Karin—in the house helps, for she feels an instinctive bond with another Asian immigrant learning to be American. Du, however, will not verbalize the complex of emotions—sexual as well as maternal—he feels for Jasmine. She has forced herself to have Bud's baby, but he has developed a dependency complex that she finds stifling. Moreover, he seems not to be interested in her except as an exotic, though her "genuine foreignness frightens" him (*Jasmine,* 26), and he appears intent on remaking her in his own image by calling her, in a colonizing move, Jane. Or, as he puts it jokingly when they first get to know each other, "Me Bud, you Jane. . . . Jane as in Jane Russell" (*Jasmine,* 26). Her confidence in herself falters, and she begins to think that Karin was right in comparing her to a tornado, for she had "created confusion and destruction" wherever she had gone (*Jasmine,* 215). Shaken, she asks herself as she hits another low in her life: "How many more shapes are in me, how many more selves, how many more husbands?" (*Jasmine,* 215).

Throughout the narrative Jasmine underscores the problems she has in her Jane Ripplemeyer reincarnation. But her narrative is almost always one of "pain and hope, hope and pain" (*Jasmine*, 225), and just when we are able to understand the extent of her unhappiness in Iowa, she gets a feeler of hope from Taylor. As if in response to her renewed wanting, he sends a card to her telling her that he and Duff are heading her way and warns her not to run away from him again. Although a part of her cautions her not to give up the duty and prudence she has been showing in her relationship with Bud, what excites her is the thought that Taylor would rescue her from the morass her life has become in Baden, and that she would be able to relive "the headiness, dizziness, *porousness*" she had experienced twice before in her life—once with Prakash, and then with Taylor in New York City (*Jasmine*, 211).

At the conclusion of *Jasmine*, then, the protagonist has to make a decision: Will she continue to be Jane Ripplemeyer and accept Bud's offer of marriage as well as bear his child, or will she run away into the future again with Taylor as Jase? Du shows her the way by abandoning her and Bud to join his sister and her family in California. Also, she comes to realize that "the world is divided between those who stay and those who leave" (*Jasmine*, 228). She understands, too, that "a brave new world" has come into being, changing even agrarian and conservative Iowa, and in that world bold decisions have to be made (*Jasmine*, 229). In addition, it occurs to her that the blind submission to fate preached by the Punjabi astrologer ages ago is no longer acceptable. Taylor's arriving with Duff reminds her of her most important American lesson: "It's a free country" (*Jasmine*, 239). And so she abandons the mask she had put on to be Jane, embraces the frontier values of "adventure, risk, transformation" (*Jasmine*, 240), and, like Huck Finn at the end of his classic tale, wanting to be adopted by none, lights out for what is her equivalent of Huck's Territory—California. She has given being civilized according to other people's norms a shot and has found that she would rather be self-responsible.

The character of Jasmine, it will now be clear, has been created to depict Mukherjee's belief in the necessity of inventing and re-inventing one's self by going beyond what is given and by transcending one's origins. For Mukherjee, immigration—specifically immigration to America—is a crucial step to be taken in any move to remake oneself in the light of one's desires. Clearly, also, the Jasmine of the novel, like the Jasmine of *The Middleman* story or Maya Sanyal of "The Tenant," is someone who is ready to go beyond conventional morality to seek fulfillment. These are all women who in the process of inventing themselves "survive and revise as best as they can" (*Jasmine*, 23). If in the process of re-creating themselves, they have to go beyond morality, they will do so. Jasmine, thus, agonizes for a while, but in the end she leaves Bud. In other words, Mukherjee has made Jasmine "lovable, but . . . not moral in the conventional sense. She's moral in her own way. She knows what's right and wrong for her. But she does end up being a tornado who leaves a lot of debris behind" (1990 interview, 25).

In shaping *Jasmine* as an immigrant bildungsroman (Grewal's phrase), Mukherjee has taken care to embed her protagonist's story within the stories of other immigrants in America. All of them are shown to be struggling to cope with America, but Mukherjee is careful to distinguish between those who have the spirit to survive and prosper in America and those who are bound to end up in frustration or are never going to adjust to the country. There can be little doubt, for instance, that Du Ripplemeyer, like Jasmine herself, will ultimately triumph in America. He is tough and resilient like her; like her, too, he is an avid learner, and he certainly knows his mind. As his high school teacher tells Jasmine, he is "in a hurry to become all American" and is "a quick study" (*Jasmine*, 28–29). This is an observation that makes Jasmine reflect on the secret of the successful immigrant: "We're all quick studies. . . . Once we start letting go—let go just one thing, like not wearing our normal clothes, or a turban or not wearing a tika on the forehead—the rest goes on its way down a sinkhole" (*Jasmine*, 29).

In some ways, of course, Du's experience of Vietnam and the rush to adjust to America have scarred him for life. He is seen, for example, as a voyeur who snoops into the bedroom where Jasmine makes love to the paralyzed Bud, somewhat like the emotionally maladjusted Shawn Patel of the story "Saints." Having to survive on his own at an early age has also made him a "materialist," a hoarder (*Jasmine*, 30), a specialist in "recombinant electronics" (*Jasmine*, 156) because he has "a genius for scavenging, adaptation, appropriate technology" (*Jasmine*, 155). He seems destined to distinguish himself in engineering school as Asian immigrants in America have recently tended to do, but at the conclusion of the novel he decides to abandon his studies for a while to help settle his sister and her family in California. In the end Du seems to have been made conscious—and this is how he is different from Jasmine—that he is a "hybrid," unlike Jasmine, whose "transformation has been genetic" (*Jasmine*, 222).

While Jasmine seeks total assimilation, and Du seems to be heading for a hyphenated existence as a "Vietnamese-American," the road Mukherjee deems to be the one definitely not to be taken by any one emigrating to America is that of the Vadheras. Although Professor Vadhera is the source of inspiration for Prakash's bid to study in America—he had written to his favorite student urging him to come and prosper in America—he himself has opted for the life of an expatriate and has holed up himself and his family in a crowded flat in Queens. His life in America has given him economic security, but it is very much a diminished thing, and he is living a lie, for he passes himself off as a professor but is really an "importer and sorter of human hair" (*Jasmine*, 151). Mrs. Vadhera thinks she is living in heaven, but what Jasmine sees is a life lived behind "ghetto walls" (*Jasmine*, 145).

The Vadheras have no commerce with the America outside their ghetto; delight to them consisted of watching Indian films on video or visiting other Indian families in their apartment building or bathing in nostalgia. In his drunken moments, the Professor complains that the stress of his job was killing him, while his parents who stay with him lament that they were "doomed to die" in a country where no one had time for them (*Jasmine*, 148). It is no wonder that Jasmine feels "immured" in Flushing and is convinced that she was "a prisoner doing unreal time" in the Vadhera flat, "prevented from breaking into the future" (*Jasmine*, 148). The Vadheras, Jasmine could see, were merely doing time in America; the professor's attitude is that he "needed to work here, but he didn't have to like it. . . . His real life was in an unlivable land across oceans. He was a ghost, hanging on" (*Jasmine*, 153). Such a life, Mukherjee seems to be saying, is bound to be frustrating, a dead end for someone wanting to reinvent herself and plunge into America, and that is why Jasmine rejects it so decisively.

As in *The Middleman*, Mukherjee takes special care to emphasize how we now live in a world where "whole peoples are on the move" (*Jasmine*, 102). It is not only Asians who are moving in large numbers to America, but within America also society is in a state of flux. In the 1980s, for instance, almost everyone seems to be heading for California: Taylor, Jasmine, Du, even old Iowans such as Carol Lutz, one of Bud's neighbors. It is impossible to remain provincial or aloof in the face of a revolution in global telecommunications and worldwide diasporas. If North America was being transformed by Asians, a country such as India was also registering the impact of the movement across continents. In small cities in Punjab, "everyone had a close relative in Canada or the United States bringing back the latest gadgets" (*Jasmine*, 88). As Jasmine puts it, "Fates are so intertwined in the modern world, how can a god keep them straight?" (*Jasmine*, 15).

In America the new immigrants run the gamut from specialist physicians to farm hands to care givers. "Poke around in a major medical facility," Jasmine opines, "and suddenly you're back in Asia" (*Jasmine,* 32). Mukherjee is very knowledgeable in this novel as in her previous collection about legal and illegal routes to America: Jasmine's narrative mentions INS raids on Mexican illegals in Texas; it reminds us of "boat people" such as Du, and Jasmine herself has firsthand experience of "the shadow world" of illegal immigration throughout the world and knows what it takes to get a fake green card in New York City. Indeed, in describing the flight Jasmine takes to Amsterdam before boarding a ship that will land her in North America, Mukherjee inserts a long rhetorical passage on "the outcasts and deportees, strange pilgrims visiting outlandish shrines . . . the wilted plumage of intercontinental vagabondage" (*Jasmine,* 101). Jasmine recollects that when she wanders out of the Florida motel after killing her rapist, she had to spend nearly a day before she saw an "American" (*Jasmine,* 129). Her first impression of New York is that it was "an archipelago of ghettos seething with aliens" (*Jasmine,* 140). Even Iowa has a Vietnamese network and is home to Hmongs, mountain people from Vietnam.

One other major theme that *Jasmine* shares with the stories of *The Middleman* is the way older Americans themselves are being changed by the influx of Asian immigrants to their country since the 1970s. For some Americans the appeal of a Jasmine is the appeal of the East: she is mysterious, inviting, and worth possessing. Significantly, unlike Taylor, Bud has no interest in Jasmine's past; he is fascinated only by her foreignness. His relationship with her makes him realize, however, that Asia was more than "a soy-bean market," and he is transformed by her enough to adopt Du to make up for "fifty years of 'selfishness'" (*Jasmine,* 14). Both Lillian Gordon and Ma Ripplemeyer are like Bud in that they would rather not hear about Jasmine's past; both, however, have the instincts of Good Samaritans and are eager to help illegal immigrants settle down in America. Lillian Gordon sees herself as "a facilitator who made possible the lives of absolute *ordinariness*" that someone like Jasmine "ached for" (*Jasmine,* 131). In fact, Lillian Gordon stretches her neck out to help undocumented aliens and lands up in jail for her efforts, even though Jasmine will always see her as someone who "represents the best in the American experience and the American character" (*Jasmine,* 137). Taylor, of course, reaches out to Jasmine for what she is, and at the end of the novel he becomes for her "the promise of America" (*Jasmine,* 240). Union with him, we can assume, will allow Jasmine both the family life and romance she craves as well as the freedom to be herself.

Mukherjee, however, is careful to show that not all older Americans are pleased about the new immigrants or are willing to embrace with open arms the Asian Americans in their midst. The captain of the shrimper who smuggles Jasmine and other illegals into Florida and then rapes her, for example, thinks of his trade as "a nigger-shipping bizness" (*Jasmine*, 111). Like Jeb Marshall of "Loose Ends," he seems to have brought nothing but contempt for Asians from his years in Vietnam. Similarly, the drunk in the bar who calls her a whore when she is out with Bud appears to have picked up his views on Asian girls from his army days when he spent too much time with bar girls in Southeast Asia.

Jasmine differs from *The Middleman* in the way it manages to go beyond the immigration theme in its portrait of white Americans. We get fairly full portraits of people such as the Hayeses and Bud Ripplemeyer; Mukherjee also peoples her novel with a number of minor characters who represent older Americans and who are interesting in themselves as well as in their relationships with Jasmine. One such character is Karin Ripplemeyer, the woman Bud has left for the protagonist. She is, understandably, resentful of Jasmine throughout the narrative and is still in love with Bud. Ironically, she manages "Karin's Hot Line" to help people under stress, although she seems to be barely able to control her emotions about Bud and Jasmine. To her credit, however, she hangs around and appears ready to pick up the pieces of her marriage when Jasmine finally abandons Bud. Unlike Karin, Kate Gordon-Fieldstein is entirely enthusiastic about Jasmine. A professional photographer in New York, Kate seems to have inherited her mother's instinctive sympathy for the homeless as well as her spirituality. Then there is Darrel Lutz, a 23-year-old neighbor of the Ripplemeyers who is under considerable pressure because of the state of his finances. He is another of Jasmine's admirers and would like her to leave with him for New Mexico to help him begin his life anew there. Near the end of the novel Darrel's inability to carry on with the farm left to him by his parents and Jasmine's unwillingness to join him lead him to kill himself in a gruesome fashion.

Darrel Lutz's grotesque death is one last reminder of the ubiquity of violence in Jasmine's life. Her experience of violence begins as a seven-year-old when she is hit hard by the astrologer and falls, biting her tongue and getting a scar in her forehead in the process. Later, in a bloody encounter, the young Jasmine kills a mad dog that is about to attack her and her companions in her Punjabi village fields. Her father has died horribly, too, after being gored by a bull. Masterji, the progressive-minded schoolteacher who had encouraged Jasmine to continue with her education, is killed by the Khalsa Lions, Sikh terrorists who are, of course, also responsible for the murder of Prakash. Jasmine is raped by the ship captain and manages to kill him. Bud is paralyzed by a shot fired by a client whose violence prefigures Darrel's suicidal act. The Iowa of the novel is as violent and as unstable as the Punjab region where Jasmine lived till her teens. So pervasive is Mukherjee's use of violence in this and other works that Brinda Bose considers it a leitmotiv of her fiction. Bose is surely right in pointing out that in all of her novels, Mukherjee has shown violence as inescapable in "the transformation of character," and that, if anything, the level of violence has gone up with succeeding novels (Bose, 73).

Mukherjee's use of violence as a motif in her third novel is the specific subject of Samir Dayal's "Creating, Preserving, Destroying: Violence in Bharati Mukherjee's *Jasmine*." Dayal notes that Jasmine herself makes the crucial comment about the role of violence in her narrative: "There are no harmless, compassionate ways to remake oneself. We murder who we were so we can rebirth ourselves in the image of dreams" (*Jasmine*, 29). Dayal also reminds us of the aptness of the epigraph Mukherjee has chosen from James Gleick's *Chaos*: "The new geometry mirrors a universe that is rough, not rounded, scabrous, not smooth. It is a geometry of the pitted, pocked, and broken up, the twisted, tangled, and intertwined." As Dayal observes, violence is done to Jasmine at certain junctures of her life, but she is also an agent of violence in some other instances. She comes to know about political violence in Punjab and about domestic violence in both Punjab and Iowa, as when she records as if in passing the actions of a nameless Osage, Iowa, man who "beat his wife with a spade, then hanged himself in his machine shed" (*Jasmine*, 156). Dayal's comment on this episode is very perceptive: "This catastrophic violence that lies just beneath the skin of the quotidian is meticulously but offhandedly catalogued by Jasmine, as though to banalize it, as though the victims, the perpetrators, and the observers of the violence were benumbing or anaesthetizing themselves against an excess of reality."[10]

Jasmine continues to reflect Mukherjee's concern with the lives of Indian women, whether battered by their husbands or leading unfulfilled lives. Almost as soon as the novel begins, the astrologer who gleefully predicts widowhood for the heroine also admonishes her to "go join your sisters [because] a girl shouldn't be wandering here by herself" (*Jasmine*,

4). By making her heroine triumph over widowhood and by depicting her opting for a fate different from what seemed to be in store for her sisters, Mukherjee is making a kind of feminist statement in the novel: women can make a difference in their lives even if they cannot cheat fate completely. As if to underline her heroine's achievement, Mukherjee draws attention repeatedly to the plight of women in Punjab: this is where a woman may look old at 21, where daughters are considered a curse, where men prefer wives who have no minds of their own and think of them as important only because they can look after the house and give birth to bright or industrious sons, where being a widow was tantamount to a sentence of life-in-death, and where women stick together when out in the fields to ward off "rape, ruin, shame" (*Jasmine,* 55).

Even Prakash is protective about Jasmine and will keep some secrets from her to shield her from unpleasant realities, although Mukherjee clearly indicates that Indian men like him had begun rethinking the rights of a woman. After all, he teaches her that "only in feudal societies is the woman still a vassal" (*Jasmine,* 77) and instructs her on leading life as a city woman and on resisting demands made on her body until she was ready to meet them. In Flushing, Jasmine confronts again the patriarchal code that required of Indian women "submission, beauty, innocence" (*Jasmine,* 151)—qualities that have made someone like Mrs. Vadhera ignorant even of the workplace where her husband can be reached in the case of a family emergency. The life Mrs. Vadhera and the women in the Indian ghetto live is undoubtedly one more reason that Jasmine is so desperate to break away from the Indian society of New York. Bud, of course, sees her only as someone who can fulfill his needs, either because she is a beautiful young woman when he first meets her or because she is such a good nurse when he is paralyzed. Nevertheless, Mukherjee has gone out of her way to distance herself from American feminists in her portrayal of Jasmine by making her not only into someone who ultimately wants to do the right thing for herself no matter what that will do to others, but also into someone who tries very hard to please others and be as feminine as possible.

Jasmine, then, embodies all the major themes that attracted Mukherjee as a writer in the past and is the climax of the literary voyage that has transformed her from a chronicler of exile to a champion of immigration. The novel is technically more ambitious than all her previous works, however, in that Mukherjee has abandoned in it the linear narrative that she used in her earlier fiction and has chosen what Gurleen Grewal has accurately (albeit unenthusiastically) described as "nonlinear narrative techniques of montage and jump-cuts, shuffling us back and forth in time" (Grewal, 187). For the most part, Jasmine, in her reincarnation as Jane Ripplemeyer, intersperses details of her present strained and unhappy life as Bud Ripplemeyer's common-law wife in Iowa with the series of events starting with the astrologer's advice to the seven-year-old Jyoti in Punjab to Bud's shooting by his aggrieved client. Chapter 1 takes us back from Elsa County, Iowa, to "lifetimes ago" in Hasnapur, India. Chapters 2 to 5 depict Jane Ripplemeyer's life in tense, economically depressed Iowa. Chapters 6 to 17 follow Jasmine from Punjab to Florida as she grows up as Jyoti and becomes Jasmine, bride and widow, and then recounts the violence done to her by the grotesque ship captain and her violent revenge on him in Florida. Chapter 18 alternates between a lunchtime encounter that Jasmine has with the white American professor at the University Club of Dalton, Iowa, who has become a believer in the Hindu concept of reincarnation, and her dazed movements as she wanders into Lillian Gordon's trailer park, where she will get a new life. Chapters 19 and 20 shuttle back and forth between the narrative present (Jasmine's life as Jane) and her Americanization by Lillian Gordon and life with the Vadheras. Chapter 21 consists of an Iowa scene. Chapters 22 and 23 take Jasmine via Kate's studio to the Hayeses. Chapter 24 begins with the scene where Bud is hit by a bullet and then goes further back to Jasmine's courtship period with Bud but mentions a letter from Taylor that suggests the possibilities of a life other than that with Bud. Chapter 25 brings us back to the narrative present where Bud is asking her to marry him. In chapter 26 Taylor arrives to rescue her and she takes another plunge into the future. All this moving backward and forward is done naturally; Mukherjee captures the fluidity of oral narratives where events are foretold and told and where past, present, and the future intermingle. Moreover, and as Pushpa N. Parekh has stressed in her study of the telling of the tale, Mukherjee oscillates skillfully "between the fluidity of voicing through self-reflection, interior monologue, and figurative language, mythologizing her new experience through the oral medium of creating 'new proverbs' to the strain of unvoicing through narrative pauses, mental blocks, and silences by volition."[11]

Mukherjee is to be credited also for giving Jasmine a voice that conveys something of the "scabrous" quality of her experience as well as the energy and hope that carries her forward through her eventful life. The unpleasantness of her Hasnapur life, for instance, is well caught in the description of the rotting body of a small dog that she finds on a riverbank; the body "broke in two, as though the water had been its glue," the moment she touched it, emitting in the process a "stench [which] leaked out" of it (*Jasmine*, 5). The landing in Florida is depicted in a tone that suggests that there is a process of demystification going on: America here is not the promised land, for the Florida beach is "Eden's waste: plastic bottles, floating oranges, sodden boxes, white and green plastic sacks tied shut but picked open by birds and pulled apart by crabs" (*Jasmine*, 107). The account of the international underworld of illegal immigrants, however, pulsates with hope, as does the details of the New York studio of Kate or the apartment of the Hayeses, where the very clutter of things seems to be full of the promise of America.

Despite the abundance of detail in the narrative, though, Mukherjee has claimed that *Jasmine* is not "a realistic novel" and was meant "to be a fable" (1990 interview, 8). This will strike some as disingenuous, for surely the novel is full of realistically staged scenes, and Mukherjee does pay close attention to setting and psychological realism. By attempting to deflect attention from the realistic moments of the novel, however, Mukherjee seems to be trying to forestall criticism of the tone with which she portrays certain aspects of Indian society and culture. More than one critic has, in fact, objected to her details about Indian life and has accused her of misrepresentation. The most comprehensive of the indictments of Mukherjee's depiction of India and the lives of Indian immigrants in America is Gurleen Grewal's essay; her litany of complaints against *Jasmine* includes the implausibility of a story line that requires Jasmine to travel from Punjab to Florida to commit *sati*; the "incomprehensibility" of Jasmine's desire to commit *sati*; the contradiction in her character where she can show a surfeit of "a will to live" at one point and can become a tabula rasa for Americanization at another; the improbability of the move from the Flushing ghetto to Manhattan, and the unbelievable ease with which an immigrant au pair can become the self-possessed common-law wife of an Iowa banker. Indeed, what Grewal basically accuses Mukherjee of is writing a willed narrative and erasing "the history and ethnic identity of the immigrant woman" and ignoring "the realities of race and class distinctions in American society" (Grewal, 186, 188, 192).

Jasmine, in other words, has drawn fire for simplifying and misrepresenting the lives of immigrant women, but it was also widely praised when it was published. It was the first of Mukherjee's books to have been reprinted the very year of its publication by the Paperback Book-of-the-Month Club, and it made the *New York Times Book Review*'s list of the year's recommended fiction. Grewal's essay was one of four essays read in a special session of the 1991 Modern Language Association, "Bharati Mukherjee and the Immigrant Tradition," devoted entirely or in part to this novel. Even though three of these four essays were unsympathetic and even hostile to the novel, the attention given to it was a measure of the attention it and its author had received ever since its publication. In fact, with the publication of *The Middleman and Other Stories* and *Jasmine* in successive years, Mukherjee had ensured that she could no longer be ignored in the contemporary American fiction scene and that she would from now on be considered a "major" American writer writing about a distinct and important theme in American fiction: the exuberance of Asian-Americans as they attempted to immerse themselves in the culture of the United States.

Chapter Five

A Hunger for Connectedness

In 1991 Bharati Mukherjee, by this time widely acknowledged as a major American writer, contributed the essay "A Four-Hundred-Year-Old Woman" to the volume *The Writer on Her Work*. In this essay Mukherjee emphasizes clearly and forcefully her literary agenda: she wants the American reading public to accept her as an "American writer, in the American mainstream, trying to extend it" ("Woman," 24). Confident that she has left behind the phases of exile and expatriation, Mukherjee formulates the task ahead of her: "Make the familiar exotic; the exotic familiar" ("Woman," 25). Mukherjee, however, is aware that in achieving her goals she must "redefine the nature of *American* and what makes an American," since, all too often, older Americans tended to think of the Asian immigrants who had been settling in North America in the 1970s as a group distinct from them because of their histories, languages, and appearances ("Woman," 25).

One way in which Mukherjee feels she could convince older Americans that their destinies were never that distinct from the new immigrants in their midst is to remind them of their historical linkage to South Asia. As "a four-hundred-year-old woman, born in the captivity of a colonial, pre-industrial oral culture, and living now as a contemporary New Yorker," Mukherjee considers herself to be in a unique position to persuade her readers of her "sense of the interpenetration of all things"— something that her study of the Mughal miniature paintings of India has also taught her ("Woman," 26). Something else Mukherjee believes she could take from Indian culture for use in the country she has made her own and intends to transform through her work is the form of the typical Indian myth, which depends on "shape-changing, miracles, godly perspectives" ("Woman," 25).

In the course of "A Four-Hundred-Year-Old Woman," Mukherjee describes her current project, "a major work, historical in nature, that nevertheless incorporates a much earlier version" of her basic project, "the making of new Americans" ("Woman," 26). In the essay she mentions that she had contracted to complete the book in the next three years. In fact, the book was published in September 1993 as *The Holder of the World* and does seem to embody all the goals she had set for herself in the essay. It is thus a novel deliberately written to extend the mainstream of American writing. It is obviously designed to redefine for her readers the meaning of America and what it meant to be an American. It is structured to emphasize the links between North America and South Asia, which, as far as Mukherjee is concerned, go as far back as the founding of the Massachusetts Bay Colony, and it is motivated by an aesthetic dependent on the sense of the interpenetration of all things and a belief in miracles and metamorphoses.

A quick summary of the plot of *The Holder of the World* indicates to what extent Mukherjee tried to meet the goals she had set for herself in "A Four-Hundred-Year-Old Woman." But it is really more accurate to talk about the *plots* of the novel, for it has a main plot and a subsidiary plot. The subsidiary plot tells the story of Beigh Masters, the novel's narrator. Beigh is a very modern, very sophisticated, 32-year-old woman, making a living as an "asset hunter," which is something of an euphemism for a job that involves ferreting out antiques and art treasures for rich collectors interested in the most elusive, and therefore the most precious, art objects. Beigh has a lover, a brilliant computer scientist named Venn Iyer, whose family came to the United States from South India and settled in the Boston area. Venn works in an MIT lab for "a virtual-reality project"—that is, a project that involves feeding data into a computer to re-create a segment of time that has passed. Specifically, throughout the novel, Venn works to enable time travel to Kansas City on the afternoon of 29 October 1989. Beigh is intrigued by his project and near the end of her narrative actually does the time traveling for him. But Beigh's job is to track down for a client a diamond called the Emperor's Tear, reputedly the most perfect diamond in the world, and she travels from Boston to India and back again in search of the priceless object supposed to have been lost while in the possession of Emperor Aurangzeb, the last of the great Mughal emperors who ruled India for two centuries.

The main plot of *The Holder of the World,* however, has to do with the strange and surprising adventures of Hannah Easton, a New Englander who was born in Brookfield, Massachusetts, to Edward and Rebecca Easton in 1670. Edward Easton died of a bee sting a year later, and Hannah's chief memory of Rebecca Easton is of the moment when she arranged for Hannah to be left with a neighbor so that Rebecca could fly away to her Nipmuc Indian lover. Instead of turning her against her mother, though, the episode keeps stimulating Hannah to go beyond the strict parameters imposed by Puritan society. Consequently, although she grows up as the adopted child of a devout Puritan couple, Robert and Susannah Fitch, she readily agrees in 1692 to marry the dashing Irish adventurer Gabriel Legge, mainly because he appears to be the type who could take her into the unknown. And so, after a couple of years in England, where she has to stay while he goes out on his adventures, she finds herself in the Coromandel coast of southeastern India as the wife of the East India Company man Gabriel has become.

Eventually, Gabriel, always irrepressible and basically the type who will not be domesticated, turns pirate and leaves Hannah to fend for herself in India. Hannah ends up with an Indian lover, a Hindu raja named Jadav Singh. For a while she experiences with the raja the kind of bliss she associates with Rebecca Easton and her Nipmuc Indian lover. But the raja is embroiled in a struggle with the mighty Mughal emperor, and love only makes him an easier prey for the ascetic, driven Aurangzeb. Hannah makes a desperate plea to the emperor to desist from destroying the raja and his kingdom. The emperor, predictably, is unmoved, and when Jadav Singh dies, Hannah finds her way back to Salem, where she takes along Pearl, the daughter she has had because of her affair with the raja.

The main plot and the subsidiary plot are linked through Beigh Masters, who in her quest for the Emperor's Tear has come across a series of Mughal miniature paintings in a maritime trade museum in Massachusetts that feature "a yellow-haired woman in diaphanous skirt and veil," who has become legendary as "Salem Bibi" or the mistress from Salem. Beigh, understandably, is intrigued by the presence of a blonde woman from New England in seventeenth-century India, the more so since in one painting of the series the blonde seems to be holding the Emperor's Tear while sharing the canvas with a vanquished raja and a gloomy emperor. Beigh's instinct tells her that Salem Bibi was Hannah Easton, and so she embarks on two quests: she will not only find out where the Emperor's Tear could have disappeared to but will also reconstruct the sequence of events that transformed Hannah Easton into Salem Bibi and made her come back to New England after having loved a raja and after having consorted with the mighty Mughal Aurangzeb. Beigh Masters finds herself more drawn, however, to "Hannah Easton Fitch Legge aka the Bibi from Salem" (the name changes, as in *Jasmine,* are significant)[1] than to the story of the diamond—so much so that she "couldn't care less about the Emperor's Tear" by then (*World,* 19). From this point on she spends over a year of

her life assembling the facts that will enable her to reconstruct the trajectory of Hannah's life and will satisfy her intense desire to know more
about the intrepid seventeenth-century woman who appeared to have
led such a fabulous life.

Even the bald summary of the two plots of *The Holder of the World*
indicate how closely the novel sticks to the agenda Bharati Mukherjee
announced for her writing in "A Four-Hundred-Year-Old Woman."
Beigh's patient reconstruction of Hannah's story is meant to suggest
that there were passages to and from India even in colonial New
England and that lives have been lived across cultures in all centuries.
Moreover, Mukherjee seems to be telling her readers that if we care to
gather the stories interspersed in history, we will come to realize how
intertwined lives are. To say that the West was West and the East was
East and that the two had scarcely met or will ever meet is an excessively
reductive and even static view of history. On the contrary, Mukherjee is
bent on demonstrating through her novel a conception of history articu-
lated in the novel through Venn, who observes that "everything in history . . . is as tightly woven as a Kashmiri Shawl" (*World,* 189). Through
Hannah Easton's life, Mukherjee will strive to make the point that even
a woman born in colonial New England could have internalized India
and Indians into her psyche in a positive way.

Indeed, what a summary of the two plots of *The Holder of the World*
fails to bring out fully is the extent to which Mukherjee shows races
interacting with each other across space and time. Beigh Masters, for
example, at first appears to have little in common with Hannah Easton
except her New England background and an Indian lover. But as she
gets more and more involved with Hannah's life, she begins to discover
other significant points of contact. Beigh finds out, for instance, that
Hannah's mother was a cousin of her own ancestor. "Vaguely then," she
was part of Hannah's story, "the Salem Bibi . . . part of the tissue" of her
own life (*World,* 21). But more significant is Beigh's discovery of the kinship of spirit that she has with Hannah. Both of them, she realizes, are
impelled by curiosity and romance, a thirst for the unknown and for a
passion that could transform their lives; both have a "hunger for connectedness" (*World,* 11). Hannah, like her mother, is drawn to the
Nipmuc Indian culture, quite unlike their fellow Puritans. Similarly,
Beigh has a very untypical interest in Indian culture, philosophy, and
lives that extends beyond what is required of her in her job or by her
affair (Venn, after all, appears to be as North American as he is South

Asian). Like Hannah, too, Beigh takes "sheer pleasure . . . in the world's variety" (*World,* 104).

Undoubtedly, part of Beigh's skills in representing Hannah's life comes from her training at Yale, where she took a seminar in Puritan history that required her to acquire the archival skills necessary "to deconstruct the barriers of time and geography" (*World,* 11). Nevertheless, it is Beigh's increasing identification with Hannah and her "hunger for connectedness" that propel her on in her quest to unravel the details of Salem Bibi's life. Not only does Beigh try to see what Hannah saw, to think and feel what she thought and felt, she also begins to project her own life onto the seventeenth-century woman's life. Always, Beigh makes us aware of the points of contact between her and her distant ancestor. Beigh tells us, for example, that she has come to a meaningful affair, as Hannah did with the raja, circuitously, for she went through "ten years of bobbing in the tangle and clutter of semiserious relationships" (*World,* 34) before she met Venn. Indeed, Beigh lets us know that her quest for Hannah is also a "kind of love song" to Venn; in piecing together the fragments that she has found of Hannah's relationship with an Indian ruler, Beigh makes us aware that she is trying to consolidate her own relationship with Venn by going to his roots to bring out "the parts of him" that she "can't reach" and by exposing to him "the parts of me he's afraid to ask about" (*World,* 60).

In making sense of Hannah's life, Beigh is striving to make sense of her own life. Beigh's work on Hannah teaches her, among other things, to go beyond her "cynical self," her "well-trained feminist self," and to be aware of "multiple contingencies" in life (*World,* 60). Even as a modern woman, Beigh can learn to value what she thinks impelled Hannah to accompany Gabriel to India: "Her curiosity, the awakening of her mind and her own sense of self and purpose" (*World,* 89). Reconstituting Hannah's life with Venn's help will, ultimately, be far more than another job done; as she sees it, it will help her and Venn to "predict what will happen to us within our lifetime" (*World,* 91).

In the course of her search for the hidden life of Salem Bibi, then, Beigh Masters learns to treasure her relationship with Venn Iyer even more than she had at its beginning. Moreover, she herself is in a sense reconstituted by the search for Hannah and the Emperor's Tear. Clearly, the most valuable lesson she learns from her quest is the subtle relatedness of all people. And just as Hannah teaches Beigh to savor her cross-cultural connection even more, Venn guides her into a belief in design and a knowledge of "a cosmic energy that quickens and governs the universe" and touches all lives (*World,* 219), something that is central to Hindu religious philosophy. It is appropriate, therefore, that it is Venn who is able to take her on his "virtual reality" machine to the climax of her quest: an encounter with Hannah that will also reveal to her what really happened to the Emperor's Tear. Hannah apparently took the diamond from the emperor intending to give it to her trusted maid-confidante Bhagmati so that she could bury it with her after she had committed suicide to escape a life of captivity with the Mughals. When, however, the virtual-reality machine makes Beigh appear in Hannah's view, Hannah confuses the time-traveler with a composite personality based on the two people she had trusted most in her life: Bhagmati and her New England friend, Hester Manning. In a sense, therefore, the secret of the Emperor's Tear will never be disinterred—it could be in Bhagmati's grave—but, in another sense, it doesn't matter. Hannah has in intention if not in effect handed over the diamond to someone who will preserve it in her memory and keep it there as a talisman for the future. To put it somewhat differently, the Emperor's Tear will sparkle forever in Beigh's imagination as a memento of Hannah's life.

The Holder of the World is thus to be interpreted as a quest narrative written to point to American readers of this age how lives have been intertwined and can be intertwined across space and time if we are willing to let go the superficial divides that separate us and if we are willing to make an emotional investment in connecting with each other. The theme of the subtle relatedness of lives is, of course, a development of the theme of immigration that Mukherjee celebrated in the third phase of her career in that she is going beyond the recent wave of immigration from Asia to America to exult in the movement across oceans and frontiers over the centuries. As K. Anthony Appiah has observed in his enthusiastic *New York Times Book Review* of the novel, *The Holder of the World* "reminds us of the interconnections among cultures that have made our modern world" and, additionally, advocates a "vigorous" and (if need be) "bitter fusion" of peoples.[2]

Another major theme of *The Holder of the World* is that of sexual awakening through an "other" lover. This theme, too, develops ideas Mukherjee has previously used in her fiction. We remember, for example, her narratives of wives leading unfulfilled lives, on the verge but not quite able to find fulfillment through an affair with a man from another race—works such as *Wife,* "The Lady from Lucknow," or "A Wife's Story." We also remember her tales of women who have finally broken through a moribund marriage to bliss or the promise of fulfilled life through a relationship with an alien—tales such as "Orbiting" and the novel *Jasmine*. Although Beigh has experienced the ash of sterile relationships and is relishing happiness with Venn, the theme of sexual awakening through an "other" is conveyed chiefly through Hannah Easton's life—that is, the main thematic focus of *The Holder of the World* is in the romance of Hannah's relationship with an Indian raja.

Even the first view given in the novel of Hannah Easton through Beigh's scrutiny of the Salem Bibi miniatures in the Massachusetts museum hints at a woman whose movement seemed focused on contact with an "other." What Beigh sees in the Mughal painting is a woman whose "hips are thrust forward, muscles readied to wade into deeper, indigo water. But her arms are clasped high above her head, her chest is taut with audacious yearnings" (*World,* 16). The first memory of Hannah that Beigh can evoke is also of her identification with Rebecca's flight with her Nipmuc Indian lover; it is an image of fulfillment she will seek to experience in her own life for a long time.

Growing up among the ascetic Fitches in the strict Puritan community of Brookfield, Hannah has no occasion for expressing her sexuality. Only the embroidery work she takes up as an occupation gives vent to her feelings about her mother and articulate the stirrings within her: "Her embroidery gave away the conflicts she'd tried so hard to deny or suppress" (*World,* 42). Still, Hannah seeks inspiration for the future wherever she can find it. When Thomas Fitch tries to make her learn a verse from *The Bay Psalm Book,* what she remembers is the corresponding verse from Psalms 2:8 that Rebecca used to sing to her: "Desire of me, and I shall give thee the heathen for thine inheritance; and the utmost parts of the earth for thy possession." Instead of being sobered by the biblical passage, Hannah promptly "emblazoned" the verse in "colors so tropical" that it becomes obvious to anyone who sees that embroidery that it had become "the embodiment of desire" (*World,* 44). Like Hawthorne's Hester Prynne in finding an outlet for her emotions in her needlework, she is also like Hester in acquiring the skills of a nurse and becoming something of a ministering angel despite the suspicions of her fellow citizens. The Hester Prynne–like ambiguity that Hannah's life is becoming is also shown when she blurts out her sacred letter in a delirium. "I is for Independence" (*World,* 55), she cries out, even though her best friend, Hester Manning, thinks that her sick friend has in mind her mother's Indian lover.

Hannah's opportunity to leave the secure but stifling world of the Puritans comes when Gabriel Legge wanders into it. He had at first courted Hester Manning, but when she dies mysteriously, this tall and dashing man with his eye patch and countless stories of adventures shifts his attention to a woman who cannot bring him any dowry but has a wilderness in her to match his own. For her, marrying is to act like her mother, "a way of joining her by running off with a treacherous alien," even if she suspects that he is somehow responsible for the death of her best friend (*World,* 69).

Marriage to Gabriel, however, fails to fulfill her: the romance of the East he conveyed through his stories proves to be as distant from her life as a housebound wife in England as it was in Salem. Not surprisingly, then, the diary she keeps as the wife of a sailor who is frequently away makes no mention of sexual passion—a lacuna that Beigh Masters finds significant, especially since Hannah wrote "so movingly of sexual passion in her later years" (*World,* 76). When word comes of Gabriel's death at sea and a bespectacled renaissance man of science named Hubert proposes to her, she does not feel inspired to accept him, even though Hubert's plans of traveling on the Continent had excited her. Then, Gabriel turns up, proving here as elsewhere in the novel that he has a Houdini-like ability to elude death and a chameleon's characteristic of reappearing in a new guise every once in a while. In his new reincarnation he has become an East India Company officer. This time she decides not to let him leave her behind, for she has become "tired of waiting at home, of not bestirring herself in a rich world opening out at every hand" (*World,* 87). The life of romance she has hungered for seems possible if she can accompany Gabriel to India.

Although Hannah arrives in India ready to immerse herself in the sights and sounds of the Coromandel coast, she finds herself confined to the petty and hierarchical world of East India Company officials and their wives. Just as the New England Puritans had separated themselves from the American Indians, the English in India seemed to have fenced themselves off from the natives of India. The Englishman or woman appeared determined to hold "India up to inspection by the lamp of England, or of Christianity" (*World,* 104). Unlike them, Hannah keeps looking for opportunities to transform herself in contact with Indians; here, as before in her life, the paradigm she will live by is the vision of her mother transforming herself by mingling with the Nipmucs. Hannah thus wants to run "errands . . . in this vast new jungle" (*World,* 105); unfortunately for her, English officialdom keeps reining her in and curbing her instincts to go native. As one East India Company official cautions her, "It is not consistent with our interest . . .

to let the people of the land see our countrywomen yield to self-indulgence" (*World,* 110).

As before, she will be frustrated in her quest for self-fulfillment also by her husband, for Gabriel neglects her, driven as he is by his own obsessions and by wanderlust. Left to herself almost all the time, she spends her "days in a dream of sensuality" (*World,* 132). She is at this juncture of her life a woman waiting to be awoken. She takes every opportunity that comes her way to walk the back lanes of "Black Town" and to mix with the local population, even if such ventures make her vulnerable to the scandal-mongers of "White Town."

The one occasion that Beigh Masters is able to record when Hannah manages to snatch a moment of sexual bliss with her husband comes about when the chief factor of the company enrages Gabriel by casting aspersions on Hannah's encounters with an Indian merchant. Enraged, Gabriel arranges for the murder of the chief factor. Delighted by her husband's gallantry, Hannah decides to reward him by making love to him one night on a beach. This much Beigh thinks she can deduce from the fragment of a verse written by an Indian fisherboy who witnessed the couple's embrace and went on to dramatize it in a play produced on the Restoration stage.

But this moment of bliss that Hannah has with Gabriel is unusual for them, and Gabriel actually deserts Hannah immediately afterwards to turn pirate. Gabriel's departure does not devastate her; she has become used to these sudden partings from her husband. In addition, she now looks forward to being on her own, for "the Coromandel had started something as immense as a cyclone deep inside her body and mind." In a way, "to let Gabriel go was also to let herself expand" (*World,* 163). And when he leaves this time she begins to talk more freely to Bhagmati and learn from her maid about Indians and their beliefs. And what she learns in the process further increases her desire to immerse herself in the life of the subcontinent.

Eventually Gabriel returns, rich from his privateering expeditions and ready to set up a trading enclave in the Coromandel coast, which would rival the one owned by the East India Company. Although Hannah does not know it yet, he now has his own Indian mistress. It is only when a conjunction of events reveals his infidelity to her as well as shatters the fragile peace between the Mughals and the company, and when she is sure that Gabriel has drowned in a cyclone in the Bay of Bengal (Beigh's research tells her he survived it and ended life as a Muslim *fakir* or holy man in Calcutta), that she is forced to leave the company's enclave.

Led by Bhagmati from the besieged enclave, Hannah finally enters the world of the natives, fulfilling thereby a dream she had been dreaming since her childhood. And it is a world every bit as fascinating as she had imagined it to be. Everything she sees around her makes "her realize how myopic" were the residents of "White Town" (*World*, 218). Even Bhagmati is no longer an Indian maid; she now reveals herself to be a beautiful girl dedicated to keeping alive the memory of the Englishman she had loved till his death—her "other"—as well as a dedicated subject of the raja Jadav Singh, the Hindu king of a kingdom at war with Emperor Aurangzeb in South India.

Hannah Easton has, in effect, entered the world of romance, and true to the logic of romance, she now is going to have the grand affair of her life with the raja. No doubt Rebecca Easton's plunge into the arms of her Nipmuc Indian lover had made her similarly heady and disdainful of restraint and reason, for Hannah now abandons herself to the Indian king. It is love at first sight for her and sex in the first close encounter; explained only by "the brief cryptic reference" that Beigh Masters has come across in Hannah's *Memoirs*: "An angel counseled me; a fantasy governed me; bliss descends on the derangers of reason and intellect" (*World*, 228).

For a few weeks Hannah and the raja make love every night and experience the high tide of love. While her whole life has been transformed by him, and she can think of nothing else except their love, the raja comes to her for part of the night and takes her only as his white Bibi. Nevertheless, Hannah is content to be only a mistress, for she has finally "felt her own passionate nature for the first time" and has discovered "that a world beyond duty and patience and wifely service was possible, then desirable, then irresistible" (*World*, 237). What she had to repress in Puritan Salem, what marriage to Gabriel failed to bring out in her except possibly once, she experiences in the raja's palace, and in the process she comes "to understand the aggressive satiety of total fulfillment" (*World*, 237).

But the raja is in the middle of a war with the emperor, and Aurangzeb has sent a vast army and his best general to destroy the Hindu king who had become a major irritant for a man bent on building a Muslim empire in the whole of India, and passion can make Jadav Singh only much more vulnerable to a Mughal attack. Inevitably, his forces are defeated, and he himself seriously wounded. Like heroines of romances who dare all to save their knights, Hannah braves it to the battlefield to rescue the fallen raja, only to be captured by the Mughal general. She manages, however, to kill the general, rescue the unconscious raja, and bring him back to his palace. Hannah's surgical skill revives the raja, but even in the world of romance ancestral hatred proves more potent than the ministrations of love. The raja rejects her proposal to run away from the feud with the emperor. Even her disclosure that she is carrying his child will not deter him from his resolution to do battle with the emperor and avenge the wrong done to his father by the Mughal king. Finding him implacable, Hannah crosses the battle line in a desperate bid to persuade Aurangzeb to agree to peace. Aurangzeb is impressed by Hannah's determination, but he, too, will not be moved from his plans to annex the raja's kingdom to his empire.

And so the final confrontation between the two armies takes place and the raja is killed in battle. The emperor lets Hannah go back to the English zone. She heads back for Salem, giving birth to Pearl on a ship somewhere in the Atlantic. Once in Salem, she locates Rebecca Easton. With her mother and her daughter, she manages to eke out an existence in the margins of the Puritan community. Not daunted by the taunts of the people of the colony, she is content to keep alive in her memory her great romance and to nurse its fruit, Pearl. In fact, she seems to even revel in the independence she has achieved in the process of waking up to true love. It is this sense of self-worth that will enable her and her daughter to lead the chant for the freedom of the colonies from the English yoke later in her life. Ultimately, she will earn the respect of her fellow citizens for her nursing skills, "the wealth of her story-telling, the pungency of her opinions" (*World,* 285). And, according to Beigh Masters's research, no less a Salem worthy than John Hathorne, son of the notorious judge and great-grandfather of Nathaniel Hawthorne, was charmed by Hannah's company in his youth and infected by wanderlust because of it.

By inscribing Hawthorne into *The Holder of the World,* by having Beigh Masters link explicitly the "morbid introspection into guilt and depression that many call our greatest work" with Hannah's life (*World,* 286), and by taking every opportunity of associating her novel with *The Scarlet Letter,* Bharati Mukherjee is making two points: she is asking her readers to place *The Holder of the World* in the tradition of American romance inaugurated by Hawthorne and is emphasizing the historical dimension of her novel.

To take the second of these two points first, *The Holder of the World* is a historical novel, albeit one written to revise notions about American colonial history held for a long time. As Claire Messud has noted in her

shrewd *Times Literary Supplement* review of the novel, "This is an alternative history which could revise forever the imaginative relations between
immigrants and 'natives' in Mukherjee's America."[3] But it is "alternative
history" not chiefly in the sense that Mukherjee is distorting history but
in the way she is developing clues left in history that allow her to blow
up the links between America and India over the centuries.

In a brief comment recorded by Joseph A. Cincotti in his write-up on
Mukherjee in the *New York Times Book Review,* Mukherjee reveals that
she began writing the novel after she came across a seventeenth-century
Indian miniature painting in a 1989 pre-auction viewing in New York.
According to Mukherjee, what she saw in this painting, a blonde-
Caucasian woman "in ornate Mughal court dress holding a lotus
bloom," was the original stimulus for the novel.[4] She asked herself then,
"Who is this very confident-looking woman who sailed in some clumsy
wooden boat across dangerous seas and then stayed there? She had
transplanted herself in what must have been a traumatically different culture. How did she survive?" Answering these questions led
Mukherjee to look at the recorded history of colonial New England, the
East India Company, and Mughal India. Evidently, Mukherjee had
found in the process enough evidence to produce a book that suggests
that there could have been connections made between America and
India in earlier centuries—connections that can inspire connections
between cultures in our time.

It is not difficult for a reader of *The Holder of the World* to imagine
Mukherjee doing research for her book like her Beigh Masters by viewing paintings in out-of-the-way museums; attending art auctions; sifting
through catalogs; poring over birth records, tombstones, and East India
Company records; digging through archives of the Massachusetts
Historical Society; talking to people adept in the history and culture of
seventeenth-century America, England, and India; and traveling to
Salem or Brookfield or the Coromandel coast to re-create the historical
context in which she had to place Hannah Easton. Obviously, answering
the question she asked herself after viewing the Mughal miniatures also
required her to mull over the classic texts of American Puritanism, the
published captivity narratives, and the extant letters, diaries, and journals of the men and women of the period. Undoubtedly, writing this
novel required Mukherjee to assay history in her bid to create a credible
world for Hannah Easton to move in.

It is not too much to say that Mukherjee's surrogate, Beigh Masters,
has the skills of the cultural historian: she is good at uniting "people and

possessions," which is to her like "matching orphaned socks through time" (*World*, 5). Certainly, too, Beigh enjoys digging up information buried in history. But merely uncovering historical bits and pieces and reassembling them does not make an interesting narrative, not to mention a good historical novel; what makes Beigh so good in interpreting the data she has assembled and weaving it into a fascinating narrative are her personal obsessions—for instance, the thought that in uncovering the truth about Salem Bibi she was reclaiming an ancestor—and her novelistic imagination. What Beigh observes about Hannah reimagining again and again the moment when Rebecca Easton left the Puritan community to be with her Nipmuc Indian lover is also applicable to Beigh (and to the novelist) herself: "Her memory is a window, letting in the fecundity of an unformed world" (*World*, 27).

The Holder of the World is written to show that what makes a historical novel come alive is the writer's imagination. By using an extract from Keats's "Ode on a Grecian Urn" as the epigraph for each of the four parts of the novel, Mukherjee is, in fact, emphasizing the role the creative imagination plays in transforming what would otherwise be seen as silence or slow time into events and characters full of life.

Indeed, Mukherjee implicitly makes the point in her novel that the creative imagination can evoke the past much more effectively than a mechanical system of retrieval, such as the one Venn uses, where data is piled on data. That is why Beigh Masters is disappointed by the trip she takes on Venn's machine to experience the "virtual reality" of a Kansas day on 29 October 1989. Venn's time machine can take her to a moment on that date, but it cannot make that moment come alive for her. Whereas when Beigh uses the same machine to find out what happened to the Emperor's Tear, she gets a much better result because of her imaginative investment in and identification with Hannah Easton. Thus, while at the end of her trip to Kansas City on 29 October 1989 Beigh cannot see the point of Venn's project—what can be the point of going through all the trouble to "intercept a lady in her yellow jacket demonstrating faucets in a Kansas City bathroom?" (*World*, 279)—at the climax of her voyage to Hannah's Indian world on that same machine, Beigh can connect with Hannah and even speak to her in an Indian language. Significantly, Beigh has in the process what Venn observes is "a near-death experience" and has the feeling in her gut that she incubated in it "an enormous diamond" (*World*, 283).

Again and again in *The Holder of the World*, we see Beigh Masters going beyond the facts in her possession after her research is done to imagine what Hannah did, felt, or yearned for. When Hester Manning brings to Hannah the book that she says everyone was reading then, Mary Rowlandson's narrative of captivity, Beigh wonders about Hannah's reactions: "I imagine her speculations: What if Edward Easton had stayed in Lancaster? Would she and Rebecca have been taken prisoners like Mary Rowlandson, sold as slaves . . . ?" (*World*, 52). If Beigh feels frustrated from time to time because of the lack of data about a period of Hannah's life, more often than not she will try to fill in the gap by imagining what had happened to Hannah. Here is Beigh, for example, trying to evoke Hannah's first view of India from shipboard: "What must Hannah, a child totally of the North Atlantic, have thought? She had been eight-months aboard a medium-sized cargo ship, eluding pirates, weathering storms. . . . Any land, even if she'd had to swim to it, would have looked good" (*World*, 103). What Beigh goes on to say she appreciates in her heroine a page later is also a compliment that can be applied to her and to what makes her so adept at reconstructing Hannah's life: "She was alert to novelty, but her voyage was mental, interior" (*World*, 104).

This again emphasizes the point that Mukherjee appears to be underlining on all these occasions: bits and pieces of history can be brought to life only by the creative imagination. And because she is also ready to use fully the license she has as a creative writer, Mukherjee can freely invent events where no facts exist for the sake of producing her "alternative history." To take one example of the imaginative license Mukherjee takes with historical records, the moment when Hannah embraces Gabriel on the beach, we remember, is witnessed by a wide-eyed fisherboy who, eventually, makes the moment part of a heroic play called *The World Taker*, written supposedly for a Restoration audience. As an asset hunter, Beigh is proud for having used the extant fragment of the play to reconstruct this episode in Hannah's life. This is why she declares, somewhat smugly, that "an asset hunter knows when to continue digging long after economists and historians have stopped" (*World*, 161). No doubt that asset hunters and novelists—they have many similarities—have definite advantages in uncovering lives, but since no play called *The World Taker* survives in any records, isn't Mukherjee really celebrating the imaginative leap writers can make to create histories?

In writing *The Holder of the World*, then, Mukherjee, self-reflexively, is drawing attention to the considerable imaginative feat that her novel really is. As Claire Messud has observed in her *Times Literary Supplement* piece on the novel, it is "an enterprise of striking audacity," and it is obvious to anyone reading it that Mukherjee wants her readers to be aware of this (Messud, 23). In some ways, therefore, *The Holder of the World* can claim metafictional status because it contains enough comments within it to make us aware of its status as a fictional artifact.

Another audacious move Mukherjee makes in *The Holder of the World* is to appropriate a literary tradition for her book just as Beigh Masters had "appropriated an ancestor" through her research on Hannah Easton (*World,* 23). After all, by alluding explicitly to Hawthorne at the end of her work and by implicitly invoking *The Scarlet Letter* throughout, Mukherjee is trying to insert her book in the tradition of the American romance. Other narrative traditions, however, are also alluded to in the novel. Thus, in an obvious manner, Rebecca Easton's life has been designed to fit into the tradition of captivity narratives best represented by Mary Rowlandson's work. But perhaps the boldest of Mukherjee's attempts at intertextuality is the book's glance at Thomas Pynchon's *V.* Mukherjee creates the occasion for inscribing her book into the metafictional tradition of Pynchon when she has Beigh ruminate on what could have happened if Hannah had not rejected a marriage proposal from a Samuel Pynchon the year before she agreed to marry Gabriel Legge: "Her life is at the crossroads of many worlds. If Thomas Pynchon, perhaps one of the descendants of her failed suitor, had not already written *V.*, I would call her a *V.*, a woman who was everywhere, the encoder of a secret history" (*World,* 60). Passages such as this one give a whole new dimension to the project Mukherjee committed herself to in "A Four-Hundred-Year-Old Woman," where she claims, "I am an American writer in the American mainstream trying to extend it" (24). Certainly by writing *The Holder of the World* Mukherjee is quite literally trying to extend the tradition of American prose narrative so that it can accommodate her work.

If, however, *The Holder of the World* stakes Mukherjee's claim to be a writer in the American grain, she is also reaffirming through the novel her Indian inheritance. One obvious way in which she displays her Indianness in the novel is by including in it a kind of celebration of the tradition of Mughal miniature painting. The reader comes across this moment of celebration quite early in the novel when Beigh Masters encounters the five Salem Bibi miniatures in the out-of-the-way Massachusetts museum of maritime trade. Beigh is clearly exhilarated by the art of the Mughal miniaturist and comments on how "the Mughal painters still startle with the brightness of their colors and the forcefulness of their feelings" (*World,* 15). Indeed, as we have noted, Beigh embarks on her quest of Hannah Easton because she is fascinated by the subject matter of the Salem Bibi miniatures. But it is also important to realize that Beigh wants to capture in her narrative of Hannah Easton's life the style of the Mughal painter, his colorfulness and emotional exuberance.

In attempting to write in the Mughal style, as in all sorts of other ways, Beigh Masters is Mukherjee's surrogate. We remember here "Courtly Vision," the concluding story of *Darkness,* which is presented as an exegesis of a Mughal miniature and which invokes the Mughal painterly mode of "total vision" (199). In "A Four-Hundred-Year-Old Woman," too, Mukherjee had declared her intention to write in the "Mughal style" till she got it right. In this essay she points out that the essence of this style is to convey "the sense of interpenetration of all things" and that this is especially suited for her favorite theme, "the hurly-burly of the unsettled magma between two worlds" (*World,* 26).

Parts of *The Holder of the World* are attempts to capture the "Mughal Style" where "everything happens simultaneously, bound only by shape and color" (*World,* 26). A good example of this is the scene instanced twice before in this chapter of Gabriel and Hannah making love on the beach. As we noted before, the scene is recorded by the fisherboy but is retouched by Beigh in her narrative, where we see the couple embracing against the backdrop of beach fishermen "spreading torn nets across the dunes; children . . . teasing sand crabs out of their holes; gulls, crows and pariah dogs . . . picking through entrails of discarded fish" (*World,* 160). But the scene is colored by Beigh's sense of wonder, too, for she exclaims in the next line, "Twilight is so fragile in the tropics! Nightfall so sudden and unequivocal!" (*World,* 160). As in the Mughal miniature paintings, there are a number of separate foci in the scene—the couple's embrace, the fisherboy's amazement, the daily life of the people who live in the area, and Beigh's wonder—even though everything is happening at the same time for the reader.

Just as Mukherjee strives to offer an "alternative history" of colonial New England by rewriting Puritan lives and working a variation on popular Puritan forms such as captivity narratives, she tries to offer an alternative version of at least one Indian myth—the story of Rama and Sita. This story of the archetypal Hindu wife who is abducted by a demon and who literally undergoes trial by fire to prove her purity to her husband has been used by Mukherjee twice before: Dimple in *Wife* and the heroine of *Jasmine* have to contend with Sita as a role model. In *The Holder of the World* Mukherjee brings in Sita's story through

Bhagmati, who tells Hannah about Sita's trials. For Hannah, the story of Sita's captivity evokes memories of the life of Mary Rowlandson as well as her mother. While in Bhagmati's orthodox rendition of the myth, Sita "is the self-sacrificing ideal Hindu wife," Hannah fantasizes Sita in her own image, "a woman impatient to test herself, to explore and survive in an alien world" (*World*, 174–75). In effect, then, Mukherjee is suggesting an "alternative history" of Sita through Hannah's reimagining of her situation.

Here Beigh makes a comment typical of a writer in the metafictional tradition when she interrupts her narrative to comment on how "orality . . . is *a complex narrative* tradition"—a fact demonstrated by reciters of Sita's story, each of whom "indulge themselves with closures that suit the mood of their times and their regions" (*World*, 176). In one of them, offered by Dr. Padma Iyer, Venn's highly successful physician mother, Sita threw herself back into the fire to show her contempt for Rama and the oppressive patriarchal tradition that he epitomizes. In the other version, put forward by Jay Basu, a recent arrival from India and a member of the MIT team working on the virtual-reality project, Sita is asked to undergo a second trial by fire by her insecure husband. This time she refuses to prove anything to him and throws herself to the ground, where Mother Earth embraces her and confers immortality on her. Mukherjee seems to be saying through these alternative versions that contemporary Indians such as the infertility specialist Dr. Iyer or the computer scientist Jay Basu will appropriate Indian tradition and refashion it to suit their times. Mukherjee's ambitions as a writer now appear to include rewriting Indian narrative traditions as well as American ones.

The wide variety of prose styles used in *The Holder of the World* also testifies to Mukherjee's ambition to make it the most technically dazzling of her novels. Here, for example, is Beigh Masters's sophisticated, almost decadent, yuppie voice: "I picked up other men—Other men— meaning the natives of other countries whose immediate attractiveness I could judge, but nothing else about them; the codes were different" (*World*, 33). Contrast this voice with the way Mukherjee makes her prose intone in the Puritan manner in her bid to invoke the climate in which Hannah grew up: "God tests us a bit at times, but He listens; His children, seeing in the rain providential purpose, prayed for strength to survive His blank indifference" (*World*, 38). Snatches of verse and prose—some imagined and some quoted from seventeenth-century texts—color Mukherjee's narrative. On some occasions Mukherjee aims at the pithiness of the seventeenth-century essay and sounds almost

aphoristic: "Before you build another city on the hill, first fill in the pot-
holes at your feet" (*World*, 91). On other occasions Beigh Masters speaks
in the tone of a Yale graduate sharing her research with an academic
audience: "For three hundred years, young Solomon [Pynchon] has
twisted in agony, a symbol of impotence and futility. (See *Neyther Myles
Standish nor Solomon Pynchon Bee: Marriage Negotiation in Two New England
Societies* by my old Yale Professor, Asa Brownleddge)" (*World*, 57).

Sometimes, though, Beigh sounds positively lyrical as when she
attempts to capture Hannah's feelings of unfulfillment on a New
England seashore: "Winds scraped sibilant music off the moss. Hardy
columbines pushed through the tiniest cracks in the rocks. Spring grass
greened afresh between dried-out stalks of mullein" (*World*, 64).
Mukherjee can mimic the jargon of computer scientists as when she has
Beigh report that Venn is "establishing a grid, a data base. . . . In the
long run, the technology will enable any of us to insert ourselves anywhere and anytime on the time-space continuum for as long as the grid
can hold" (*World*, 7). She can also make Beigh convey the color and energy
of the Mughal style as in her description of a scene captured in a Mughal
artifact in the Massachusetts museum: "the Emperor . . . splices in the
sunlight with uncut gems. The world turns slowly now in a haze of
blood, then glitters in a sea of gold, then drowns in the lush green that
chokes his palace walks" (*World*, 9).

No doubt because Mukherjee aimed to accomplish so much in *The
Holder of the World*, she is not always able to carry out her intentions in it.
One overall problem, as Claire Messud notes so perceptively in her
review of the novel, is that "the book takes itself so seriously that it risks
becoming more interesting to think about than to read" (Messud, 23).
An example of this self-absorption is Beigh's intrusive and adulatory
comment to Hannah, "She was, she is, of course, a goddess-in-the-mak-
ing" (*World*, 163). Again and again, Beigh interrupts the narrative to
point out the significance of what is going on, thereby irritating the
reader: "wherever she [Hannah] stayed, I am convinced she could have
changed history, for she was one of those extraordinary lives through
which history runs a four-lane highway" (*World*, 189). Another symptom
of a novel that tries a little too hard to dazzle is prose that can be occasionally a little too mannered, as in the alliterative, italicized message
Salem Bibi appears to give Beigh in the maritime museum: "*Found with
me a city where lions lie with lambs, where pity quickens knowledge, where desire
dissipates despair*" (*World*, 19). Certain sentences sound too knotted or

positively grate as when Mukherjee is striving to present Puritan thought: "Devastation exfoliates providential efficacy" (*World,* 38).

Although the romance mode licenses Mukherjee to play with facts and to imaginatively reorder reality, she seems occasionally to forget that she is also writing a historical novel that demands that actions are accounted for or at the least made plausible. For instance, Bhagmati's devotion to her dead English lover's memory is in keeping with her role as a character of a romance, but how does she retain a connection with her liege lord, the raja Jadav Singh, while serving as a maid in the "White Town"? Also, the episode where Hannah watches Bhagmati returning to her bed at dawn, "a regal form . . . in a white shimmering material and gold ceinture, her ankles and wrists joining softly with gold" (*World,* 155), is never sufficiently accounted for. How does she manage to be "a servant transformed" (*World,* 155) and change roles with such impunity, and to what end does she transform herself? Mukherjee, in fact, comes close to "orientalizing" Bhagmati in such a description, for she seems to be playing on stereotypes of the mystery and sensuousness of the Orient in such a scene.

Despite such occasional lapses, *The Holder of the World* is an impressive work. It shows Mukherjee reaffirming her Indianness while asserting her Americanization. She appears to have found through this novel a way to reconcile the Indian part of her heritage with the part that wants to celebrate immigration to America. In fact, *The Holder of the World* shows a "hunger for connectedness" Mukherjee has not displayed in her previous fiction. E. M. Forster, one of the subjects of Mukherjee's doctoral dissertation and the dominant influence on her first novel, *The Tiger's Daughter,* had urged almost wistfully in his fiction, "Only connect," and in her latest novel Mukherjee tries to meet this goal. Forster's *A Passage to India* was a major influence on Ruth Prawer Jhabvala's *Heat and Dust,* a novel that is like *The Holder of the World* in consisting of two parallel stories about cross-cultural connections skillfully put together, and it is interesting to speculate if Mukherjee is extending Forster's tradition, too, through her fourth novel as she is adding on to an American one begun by Hawthorne.

Conclusion

The four novels, two collections of short fiction, and prose works Bharati Mukherjee has written to this date have made her a major presence in North American letters. But Mukherjee's work needs to be put into perspective and the value of her contribution to literature should be ascertained with care. Where, exactly, is her place in contemporary literature? And how good a writer is she?

The first thing to be said about Mukherjee in placing her in the current literary scene is that she should be seen as a writer of the Indian diaspora—that extraordinary movement of many South Indians in the twentieth century that has dispersed them throughout the world. As a writer of the Indian diaspora, Mukherjee can be placed in such distinguished company as V. S. Naipaul and Salman Rushdie. Like them, she has taken advantage of a Western education and mastery of the English language to write socially alert fiction about the transformations that are created by the westward movement of South Asians in our time.

Initially, Mukherjee seems to have modeled her career on that of V. S. Naipaul, that "accidental tourist" who has "written most movingly about the pain and absurdity of art and exile, of 'Third world art' and exile among the former colonizers; the tolerant incomprehension of hosts, the absolute impossibility of ever having a home" (*Days*, 287). Indeed, in "A Conversation with V. S. Naipaul," a panel discussion recorded for *Salmagundi,* Mukherjee identified herself as "an extravagant admirer" of Naipaul for his writing "about unhousing and remaining unhoused and at the same time [being] free."[1] This comment, significantly, was made in the "expatriate" phase of her career, the time when she was writing about South Asians leading lives of quiet desperation in the land they had emigrated to, the time of *Wife* and *Darkness.* True, Mukherjee is more positive than Naipaul even in this phase of her career, but she is like him then in writing "ironical and cautionary fictions about the uneasy passage of Asian Indians to participate in the American dream."[2]

Mukherjee, however, dropped Naipaul as a model in the "immigrant" phase of her career, for she then committed herself to celebrating the melting-pot of America. From Mukherjee's perspective, by writing the *Middleman* stories and *Jasmine,* she was casting her lot with Salman

Rushdie. As she makes clear in "Prophet and Loss: Salman Rushdie's Migration of Souls," her review-essay of his fiction, what she found appealing in him was his notion that "immigration, despite losses and confusions, its sheer absurdities, is a net *gain,* a form of levitation, as opposed to Naipaul's loss and mimicry."[3] Mukherjee links herself to Rushdie even more vigorously in "After the Fatwa," the essay she co-authored with her husband, Clark Blaise, on the beleaguered author of *The Satanic Verses.* In this essay Mukherjee declares herself Rushdie's ally because of their "shared concern about immigration from India" and distances herself even further from Naipaul, a diaspora writer of an earlier generation who is like a "gracious house guest" who never complains, unlike the rambunctious Rushdie who asserted his stake in Britain in flamboyant ways.[4] When Mukherjee sees in Rushdie's life "an upscale version of everyone's immigrant experience—freedom and celebrity gained, language, religion, community lost," she is no doubt thinking of her own gains and losses through immigration to the West.

"Prophet and Loss," Mukherjee's appraisal of Rushdie's fiction, suggests some of the points of contact between her work and his novels. She indicates in this piece that the opening of Rushdie's *The Satanic Verses,* where an Air-India jumbo jet explodes over London, hints at the Air-India plane crash over Ireland that is the basis of *The Sorrow and the Terror.* Like Rushdie, she is impelled to write about an air disaster by her interest in the immigrant condition, but whereas Rushdie's treatment of the crash is quite fantastic, Mukherjee's documentary version of it depends on what really happened as well as her feelings of pity and terror occasioned by it. Like Rushdie, although without his exuberance and his extravagance, she has tried to use Indian myths in her fiction. Her *The Holder of the World* is a little like *The Satanic Verses* in having a split narrative with two central characters. Undoubtedly, Mukherjee's works have none of the manic energy that enlivens Rushdie's books, and she nowhere blends the "allegorical, mythical, allusive, pop, topical, and satirical" as he does to produce his polyphonic novels; still, she is like him in his autobiographical renderings—"usually highly realistic—of the postcolonial and immigrant experience" ("Prophet," 11, 12). Then, too, Mukherjee's Jasmine and Hannah Easton lead lives that depend on "miraculous translations," as is the case with Rushdie's heroes in *The Satanic Verses,* although once again, it is important to note that Mukherjee's heroes have none of the grotesqueness or the eccentric energy of his creations. Finally, in *The Holder of the World* at least, Mukherjee is like Rushdie in treating history as something that could be exploited for use in the present to buttress the immigrant's attempts at reworlding.

A few critics have affiliated Mukherjee with some other, less well-known, women writers of the Indian diaspora. Roshni Rustomji-Kerns thus places Mukherjee with Santha Rama Rao and Kamala Markandaya as "South Asian women recreating in their writings, the lives of immigrants and expatriates" and depicting through their fiction "people who are caught in the awkward act of juggling with multiple cultures."[5] Concentrating on the earlier phases of Mukherjee's career, Rustomji-Kerns compares Santha Rama Rao's *Home to India* (1956) to Mukherjee's first novel, *The Tiger's Daughter*, for both books deal with the emotions of expatriate Indian women responding to a prolonged visit to their country of origin.

In "Kamala Markandaya, Bharati Mukherjee, and the Indian Immigrant Experience," Emmanuel S. Nelson compares Markandaya's 1972 novel *The Nowhere Man* with *Darkness*, finding in the two books similar records of the trauma of expatriation and the bitterness occasioned by the experience of racism. Nelson's summary of the points of contact between Mukherjee and Markandaya as writers who bring "a uniquely Indian perspective to the themes of immigrant fiction" is worth quoting in full because it also reminds us of the range of Mukherjee's interests in her fiction:

> failed quests and thwarted dreams; nostalgia for a home that exists only in memory; conditions of dislocation and isolation; marital stress and intergenerational conflicts caused by the demands of a new and hostile cultural environment; loss of a supportive community and often unsuccessful attempts to forge new support systems; crippling loss of a relatively coherent earlier identity; and painful searches for an orderly sense of self and a healing awareness of personal and cultural wholeness.[6]

Mukherjee's work thus makes her a writer of the Indian diaspora and links her to novelists who are as different from each other as Naipaul or Rushdie or, for that matter, Markandaya. But as an Indian writer who has settled first in Canada and then the United States, Mukherjee can be categorized somewhat more specifically as an Indian-American writer. This is how Craig Tapping locates her in his thoughtful essay "South Asia/North America: New Dwellings and the Past." Tapping associates Mukherjee with writers such as Ved Mehta, Rohinton Mistry, Suniti Namjoshi, Michael Ondaatje, Vikram Seth, and Sara Suleri, for, like her, they have distinguished themselves by their work in North America and have tried to "construct alternative identities and communities" in their adopted countries. Comparing Mukherjee to the Sri Lankan-Canadian Michael Ondaatje, Tapping notes how "exuberantly polyphonic" their works can become as they use their diasporic, postcolonial backgrounds in North America.[7] What Tapping deduces about Sara Suleri from *Meatless Days* (1989)—that she can never cut herself off in her writing from the country of her birth, Pakistan, despite her decision to sever her ties to it and become an American—applies in some measure to Mukherjee. Mukherjee, too, cannot but bring India into her works, even though she has announced her intention to loosen her ties to it as far back as *Days and Nights in Calcutta*.

Mukherjee is thus one of a handful of writers who represent the emerging tradition of Indo-American writing.[8] But she can also be placed in the much broader and older tradition of Asian-American literature. Certainly, by focusing attention in some of her *Middleman* stories on characters from the Philippines (Blanquita in "Fighting for the Rebound"), Afghanistan (Roshan of "Orbiting"), Iraq (Alfie Judah of "The Middleman"), and Vietnam (Eng of "Fathering"), and by connecting Jasmine's fate to her adopted Vietnamese son Du's at the end of the third novel, Mukherjee is making the point that she is representing all Asian immigrant lives in America in her fiction and not just South Asian ones. In this respect Mukherjee can be affiliated with writers such as Maxine Hong Kingston and Amy Tan, who are inspired by the sagas of Asian immigrants and committed to the Asian-American woman's struggle for self-realization and her freedom from oppressive traditions. Like these writers, Mukherjee has produced fiction where her Asian heritage is tied to her American circumstance. Mukherjee's recent fiction resembles the work of Kingston in its self-consciousness, its movement away from realism, and its blend of myth, history, and personal experience. Shirley Geok-lin Lim's comments about Kingston in "Twelve Asian American Writers: In Search of Self-Definition" will also do for a novel such as *The Holder of the World*: "Kingston's works are largely self-referential, appealing not to external historical and sociological validations but to insights that come from the confrontations of invented, historical, and biographical selves."[9]

In another essay, "Assaying the Gold; or, Contesting the Ground of Asian American Literature," Geok-lin Lim has noted how under the impact of theory and the gains made by feminism, cultural studies, and oppositional criticism in general, Asian-American writing has flowered in recent times. She notes, moreover, the impetus given to Asian-American writing by the massive increase in immigration to the United States from Asia since the revision of immigration laws in 1965. Writers such as Bharati Mukherjee, it is clear from the figures presented by Lim about the explosion of Asian immigration to America in the 1970s and the 1980s, have not only been able to draw their material from the increasingly visible Asian presence but have also gained in confidence because of it. While Lim insists that it is no longer possible to treat Asian-American culture as "a fairly homogenous system of values and common ideologies,"[10] her essay does allow us to see some of the ways in which Mukherjee's work resembles that of other Asian-American writers. For example, "the three stages of identity in relation to ethnicity" of Asian Americans that Lim deduces by analyzing the autobiography of the Filipino-American writer Carlos Bulosan's *America in the Heart* (1991)—"the pre-ethnic or Asian-national" stage, where the immigrant ruminates on his life in his native country; the "national ethnic identity" stage, where he affiliates himself with other immigrants from his country who have experienced racism in the New World; and the "post-ethnic" stage, where he identifies with a wider, transnational grouping of immigrants—are approximated in the three phases of Mukherjee's fiction (Lim, 152). As we have seen, Mukherjee began by writing about India as someone who had exiled herself from it, moved on to depict the Indian expatriate's vulnerability to racism and sense of alienation in North America, and finally made herself the spokesperson of all immigrants in America regardless of their nationality. That Mukherjee's work can be placed in a broader category linking her to the major practitioners of Asian-American writing is a point made by Lim elsewhere in this essay when she describes how "writers such as Kingston, [David] Hwang, Mukherjee, and [Cynthia] Kadohata have moved beyond the conventional dichotomous, binary constructions of white and Asian-national to a positioning of ethnic identity as interrogative, shifting, unstable, and heuristic" (Lim, 160).

It is important to keep in mind, however, that while Mukherjee has not hesitated to affiliate herself explicitly to writers of the Indian diaspora or implicitly to Asian-American writing, she has gone out of her way time and again in recent years to declare herself to be first and foremost an American writer and to denounce hyphenization. We recall the polemical Preface to *Darkness,* where she had identified herself as an "Ellis Island" writer; the Whitmanesque overtones of "Immigrant Writing: Give Us Your Maximalists!" ("I'm one of you now"); and her unequivocal assertion in "A Four-Hundred-Year-Old Woman" that "I am an American writer, in the American mainstream trying to extend it . . . not an Indian writer, not an exile, not an expatriate" but an "immigrant" whose "investment is in the American reality, not the Indian" ("Woman," 24).

As this book has indicated, Mukherjee has striven to place her work in one tradition or another of American fiction ever since *Wife*, which resembles the writing of Nathanael West and Flannery O'Connor and could be described as South Asian-American Gothic; *Darkness*, of course, declared itself to be "immigrant" fiction pace Malamud and Henry Roth; the *Middleman* is a language experiment in that it depends on the idioms of America and so carries forward a tradition in American fiction inaugurated by Melville in *Moby-Dick*'s "Call me Ishmael"; *Jasmine* ends as does *Huck Finn*, with the protagonist lighting out, so to speak, for the territory ahead; and *The Holder of the World* places itself brazenly with *The Scarlet Letter* and the tradition of American romance.

Not content with clearing a space for herself in American letters that will bring her recognition as an "American writer, in the American mainstream, trying to extend it" ("Woman," 24), Mukherjee seems at times to have ambitions to redirect the flow of contemporary American fiction. She has been open about her dissatisfaction with such recent trends as minimalism and appeared to have her own future achievement in mind when, in a panel discussion on American fiction in 1981, she praised Ruth Prawer Jhabvala for "making for herself a place in American literature and subverting the very notion of what the American novel is and of what American culture is."[11] She has explained that her quarrel with the work of Raymond Carver or Ann Beattie stems from their decision to abandon "an oceanic or social view" and their intent to concentrate on "fiction about personal relationships" or on "small disappointments" (1990 interview, 29). What she and other hybrid, postcolonial writers were bringing to American fiction, on the other hand, was "a social and political vision [which] is an integral part of writing a novel, of being a novelist" (1990 interview, 29).

To their credit, North American writers have welcomed Mukherjee to their fold and have acknowledged her claim to a place in the mainstream of American fiction. Even Canada, which she left in anger and which she has displayed as a hostile and cold country, has shown its appreciation of her work by shortlisting *Wife* for a major award and by giving her a prize for her bitter attack on Canadian immigration policies in "An Invisible Woman." And though *Darkness* did not find a publisher in the United

States and had to be first printed in Canada, it was heralded in the *New York Times Book Review*. *The Middleman,* of course, received the National Book Critics Circle Award, and *Jasmine* was chosen as one of the best books of 1989 by the *New York Times Book Review*. When *The Holder of the World* appeared, K. Anthony Appiah supported its claim to kinship with *The Scarlet Letter* by observing that the novel had earned its connection to that great work and that "Nathaniel Hawthorne *is* a relative of hers, and, like Hannah Easton, she [Mukherjee] has every right to claim her kinship across the centuries" (Appiah, 7).

But if literary America has been, on the whole, generous in welcoming Mukherjee to its midst, it is necessary to note that Mukherjee's work has, on occasions, been criticized and her perspective on immigration to America has even been denounced, especially by some Indian critics. In an essay published in *Bharati Mukherjee: Critical Perspectives,* for instance, Alpana Sharma Knippling has questioned Mukherjee's project to radicalize American fiction by bringing to it the story of people who have been hitherto unrepresented in it. As far as Knippling is concerned, Mukherjee's professed elitism—she has herself proclaimed her "top family, top caste, top city" ("Maximalists," 28) status in India—very nearly disqualifies her from representing the ordinary South Asian's immigrant experience in North America. In Knippling's view, the manner in which Mukherjee elides the difficulty of the process through which a Punjabi peasant girl like Jasmine becomes the confident "self-willing subject of the West" is indicative of the facile nature of Mukherjee's bid to represent the Other (Knippling, 150). Moreover, Knippling finds in Mukherjee's fiction a tendency to gloss over the cultural specifics of different ethnic groups and a readiness to equate the experience of a Punjabi peasant girl such as Jasmine with her adopted Vietnamese son, Du, or the Trinidadian Jasmine of the *Middleman* story. As Knippling puts it, "To thus homogenize the other (Jasmine = Du; Trinidad Jasmine = Indian Jasmine) is to discount heterogeneity as a viable condition of ethnic minorities in the United States" (Knippling, 154).

Debjani Banerjee, also in an essay published in *Bharati Mukherjee: Critical Perspectives,* indicts Mukherjee from another angle. To Banerjee, Mukherjee fails "to contextualize the historical and political events of India" and is unable to "perceive the complex workings of postcolonial and neocolonial forces" in novels such as *The Tiger's Daughter* and *Jasmine* (Banerjee, 162). Banerjee opines that Mukherjee's depiction of the turbulence of Calcutta in *The Tiger's Daughter* is vitiated by her lack of sympathy for the revolutionary ideals of the Naxalites, who saw themselves locked in a class struggle. Banerjee even discerns anxiety and paranoia in the novel, for Mukherjee seems to be haunted in it by the fear that the privileged class she is from is under siege from the revolutionaries. Banerjee articulates the dissatisfaction of many South Asians with Mukherjee's work by noting that Mukherjee represents Indians in such a way that implies "one must escape from the disillusionment and treachery of postcolonial history" (Banerjee, 170). Certainly, Banerjee has a point here, for all too often Mukherjee represents India in her fiction as if to emphasize it as a land without hope or a future. Banerjee also underscores the ease with which Mukherjee's protagonists forget their Indian past in their rush to immerse themselves in America. In sum, Banerjee accuses Mukherjee of "catering to a First World audience while still mining the Third World for fictional material" (Banerjee, 173).

Gurleen Grewal, another critic represented in *Bharati Mukherjee: Critical Perspectives,* is every bit as hostile as Banerjee in her response to Mukherjee's work, particularly to *Jasmine.* Grewal, in effect, arraigns Mukherjee for making *Jasmine* a book that propagates the American dream by overlooking the barriers of education, gender, race, and history that would have made it impossible for a Punjabi peasant girl to become a liberated and articulate New World woman in a relatively short time. Grewal also attacks the novel's author for stereotyping Indian life and for dwelling on aspects of Hindu culture for the sake of sensationalism, as when Mukherjee has Jasmine heading for Florida so that she can commit *sati* by immolating herself on the campus of her dead husband's dreams. Grewal feels that Mukherjee everywhere slights social and psychological realism in romancing with America. Grewal thinks that Mukherjee misrepresents India and simplifies the experience of South Asians in America, making her own success in America into the archetypal immigrant story, even though few immigrants share her privileged background. In Grewal's words, "to assume that unskilled, illegal women immigrants like Jasmine—who are not fluent in the English language—have the same opportunities as upper-class, educated immigrant women is to make a mockery of their lives" (Grewal, 193).

It is possible to indict Mukherjee on other counts for her portrayal of South Asia and South Asian immigrants in America in her fiction. Telltale signs such as the way Mukherjee misspells the capital of Bangladesh as "Dakha" in the *Darkness* story "Angela" or the way she dots Punjab in the 1970s with satellite dishes in *Jasmine* reveal her proneness to err in her representation of the recent changes on the subcontinent. One notices, too, how unconvincing Mukherjee is in her later fiction whenever she has an Indian speak English. Almost all of the Indians in the novels and stories she wrote in the 1980s tend to speak in the same way, perpetuating stereotypical notions about Indian English, when the truth is that the way an Indian speaks the language depends greatly on the part of the country he is from or the school she went to. In general, it appears to be the case that Mukherjee is having problems in depicting India and Indians because she has been too long in the West, and it is surely significant that her ear for "Indian English" has deteriorated at a time when she has been praised for her skills in rendering American English.

It should be said, however, that Mukherjee has continued to cultivate her ties to India and in interviews and her nonfiction has asserted again and again her belief in Hinduism and her pride in the achievements of classical Indian culture. But Roshni Rustomji-Kerns has a point when she observers that Mukherjee's "discussions of these subjects tend to have the aura of intellectual exercises" (Rustomji-Kerns, 657). It is also noteworthy that Mukherjee has almost nothing to say about blacks and the black experience of racism in America (the one black character to appear in her fiction, Washington McDowell in *The Tiger's Daughter,* is on view in Calcutta). It is as if Mukherjee is bent on ignoring the truth about racism in the United States in her bid to depict it as a country where race is never an obstacle to the fulfillment of the American dream.[12] In total contrast, we can get the feeling from reading the Canadian stories that Indian immigrants to Canada always encounter hostility or indifference, even though there are success stories to be told about them, too.

Despite such shortcomings, however, we can conclude that Mukherjee has created original and valuable fiction about the immigrant experience in North America. She has taken American fiction in new directions and can claim to be a major ethnic woman writer of contemporary America. At her best, she has been able to bring to her firsthand experience of exile, expatriation, and immigration her considerable narrative skills and a lively imagination to produce memorable and colorful tales of the excitement as well as the traumas of adjusting to a new world. Novels such as *The Tiger's Daughter* and *Wife* have the authentic stamp of experience, while stories such as "Isolated Incidents," "The World According to Hsu," and "Saints" (from *Darkness*) and "Loose Ends," "Orbiting," "The Tenant," and "The Management of Grief" (from *The Middleman and Other Stories*) can claim their place among the best short fiction coming out of America in the 1980s. Mukherjee's portion of *Days and Nights in Calcutta* is a triumph of self-examination, and an essay such as "An Invisible Woman" is a testament of an articulate, forceful, and passionate personality. And *The Holder of the World,* Mukherjee's most recent work, is proof that she has it in her to surprise us yet again with innovative and enjoyable fiction that also stresses the importance, even the inevitability, of cross-cultural connections and the subtle relatedness of us all.

Notes and References

Chapter One

    1. Geoff Hancock, "An Interview with Bharati Mukherjee," *Canadian Fiction Magazine* 59 (May 1987): 31; hereafter cited in text as 1987 interview.

    2. *Days and Nights in Calcutta,* with Clark Blaise (1977; New York: Penguin Books, 1986), 181; hereafter cited in text as *Days.*

    3. "A Four-Hundred-Year-Old Woman," *American Studies Newsletter* 29 (January 1993): 24; hereafter cited in text as "Woman."

    4. Michael Connell, Jessie Grearson, and Tom Grimes, "An Interview with Bharati Mukherjee," *Iowa Review* 20, no. 3 (Spring 1990): 9; hereafter cited in text as 1990 interview.

    5. Alison B. Carb, "An Interview with Bharati Mukherjee," *Massachusetts Review* 29, no. 4 (Summer 1988): 653; hereafter cited in text as 1988 interview.

    6. *Darkness* (New York: Penguin Books, 1985), 1–2; hereafter cited in text.

    7. "An Invisible Woman," *Saturday Night* 96 (March 1981): 39; hereafter cited in text as "Invisible."

    8. "Immigrant Writing: Give Us Your Maximalists!" *New York Times Book Review,* 28 August 1988, 1; hereafter cited in text as "Maximalists."

Chapter Two

    1. Michael Seidel, *Exile and the Narrative Imagination* (New Haven, Conn.: Yale University Press, 1986), ix.

    2. John Spurling, review of *The Tiger's Daughter, New Statesman,* 6 July 1973, 25.

    3. *The Tiger's Daughter* (Boston: Houghton Mifflin, 1971), 37; hereafter cited in text as *Daughter.*

    4. Maya Manju Sharma, "The Inner World of Bharati Mukherjee: From Expatriate to Immigrant," in *Bharati Mukherjee: Critical Perspectives,* ed. Emmanuel S. Nelson (New York: Garland Publishing, 1993), 5; hereafter cited in text.

    5. Debjani Banerjee, " 'In the Presence of History': The Representation of Past and Present Indias in Bharati Mukherjee's Fiction," in *Critical Perspectives,* ed. Nelson, 163, 166; hereafter cited in text.

    6. "Oh, Calcutta!" (review of *The Tiger's Daughter*), *Times Literary Supplement,* 29 June 1973, 736.

7. Pramila Venkateswaran, "Bharati Mukherjee as an Autobiographer," in *Critical Perspectives*, ed. Nelson, 32; hereafter cited in text.

8. When Blaise goes on in the second of these two quotes to say, "All Indians writing in English are outsiders," however, his comment appears from our contemporary perspective to be a dated one. Surely, for Indians to write in English seems nowadays to be a natural activity, and there is currently an efflorescence in Indian writing in English.

Chapter Three

1. The phrase is Krishna Baldev Vaid's in his review of the novel in *Fiction International*, no. 4–5 (1975): 156.

2. *Wife* (Boston: Houghton Mifflin, 1975), 3; hereafter cited in text.

3. Brinda Bose, "A Question of Identity: Where Gender, Race, and America Meet in Bharati Mukherjee," in *Critical Perspectives*, ed. Nelson, 55, 57; hereafter cited in text.

4. Janet M. Powers, "Sociopolitical Critique as Indices and Narrative Voice and Gender Codes in Bharati Mukherjee's *Wife* and *Jasmine*," in *Critical Perspectives*, ed. Nelson, 95.

5. Linda Sandler, "Violence as a Device for Problem-Solving" (review of *Wife*), *Saturday Night* 90, no. 5 (October 1975): 76.

6. Gita Rajan, "Bharati Mukherjee," in *Writers of the Indian Diaspora: A Bio-Bibliographical Critical Sourcebook*, ed. Emmanuel S. Nelson (Westport, Conn.: Greenwood Press, 1993), 236, 237; hereafter cited in text.

7. Rosanne Klass, "Indian Wife Lives Soap-Opera Life" (review of *Wife*), *Ms.*, October 1975, 83.

8. Jasber Jain, "Foreignness of Spirit: The World of Bharati Mukherjee's Novels," *Journal of Indian Writing in English* 13, no. 2 (July 1985): 16.

9. Martin Levin, review of *Wife*, *New York Times Book Review*, 2 January 1972, 16.

10. Liew-Geok Leong, "Bharati Mukherjee," in *International Literature in English: Essays on the Modern Writers*, ed. Robert L. Ross (New York: St. James Press, 1991), 490; hereafter cited in text.

11. Carol Stone, "The Short Fictions of Bernard Malamud and Bharati Mukherjee," in *Critical Perspectives*, ed. Nelson, 213; hereafter cited in text.

12. Anita Desai, "Outcasts" (review of *Darkness*), *London Magazine*, December 1985 and January 1986, 143; hereafter cited in text.

13. Patricia Bradbury, review of *Darkness*, *Quill and Quire* 51, no. 8 (August 1985): 43; hereafter cited in text.

14. Mitali R. Pati, "Love and the Indian Immigrant in Bharati Mukherjee's Short Fiction," in *Critical Perspectives*, ed. Nelson, 204.

15. Peter Nazareth, "Total Vision," *Canadian Literature* 110 (Fall 1986): 187; hereafter cited in text.

16. George Woodcock, "Mulberry Bush," *Canadian Literature* 107 (1985): 152.

17. Hope Cooke, review of *Darkness, New York Times,* 12 January 1986.

18. *The Sorrow and the Terror: The Haunting Legacy of the Air India Tragedy,* with Clark Blaise (Markham, Ontario: Viking Penguin, 1987), ix; hereafter cited in text as *Sorrow.*

Chapter Four

1. For a refutation of Mukherjee's claim to represent "the other" and author narratives in a radical vein, see Alpana Sharma Knippling's "Toward an Investigation of the Subaltern in Bharati Mukherjee's *The Middleman and Other Stories* and *Jasmine,*" in *Critical Perspectives,* ed. Nelson, 143–61; hereafter cited in text. I take up Knippling's critique of Mukherjee in my concluding chapter.

2. *The Middleman and Other Stories* (1988; New York: Fawcett Crest, 1989), 185; hereafter cited in text as *Middleman.*

3. Elizabeth Ward, review of *The Middleman and Other Stories, Washington Post Book World,* 3 July 1988, 9; hereafter cited in text.

4. Jonathan Raban, review of *The Middleman and Other Stories, New York Times Book Review,* 19 June 1988, 1, 23; hereafter cited in text.

5. Polly Shulman, "Home Truths" (review of *The Middleman and Other Stories*), *Voice Literary Supplement,* June 1988, 19.

6. This phrase is Jonathan Raban's (p. 23).

7. *Jasmine* (New York: Grove Weidenfeld, 1989), 241; hereafter cited in text.

8. Ralph J. Crane, "Of Shattered Pots and Sinkholes: Female Identity in Bharati Mukherjee's *Jasmine,*" paper presented at the sixth SPACLALS Triennial Conference in Freemantle, Western Australia, 9–11 December 1992; hereafter cited in text.

9. Gurleen Grewal, "Born-Again American: The Immigrant Consciousness in *Jasmine,*" in *Critical Perspectives,* ed. Nelson, 182; hereafter cited in text.

10. Samir Dayal, "Creating, Preserving, Destroying: Violence in Bharati Mukherjee's *Wife* and *Jasmine,*" in *Critical Perspectives,* ed. Nelson, 73.

11. Pushpa N. Parekh, "Telling Her Tale: Voice and Gender Roles in Bharati Mukherjee's *Jasmine,*" in *Critical Perspectives,* ed. Nelson, 111.

Chapter Five

1. *The Holder of the World* (New York: Alfred A. Knopf, 1993); hereafter cited in text as *World.*

2. K. Anthony Appiah, review of *The Holder of the World, New York Times Book Review,* 10 October 1993, 7; hereafter cited in text.

3. Claire Messud, review of *The Holder of the World, Times Literary Supplement,* 12 November 1993, 23; hereafter cited in text.

4. Joseph A. Cincotti, "Same Trip, Opposite Direction," *New York Times Book Review,* 10 October 1993, 7.

Conclusion

1. "A Conversation with V. S. Naipaul," with Robert Boyers, *Salmagundi* 54 (Fall 1981): 5.

2. C. L. Chua, "Passages from India: Migrating to America in the Fiction of V. S. Naipaul and Bharati Mukherjee," in *Reworlding: The Literature of the Indian Diaspora,* ed. Emmanuel S. Nelson (Westport, Conn.: Greenwood Press, 1992), 60.

3. "Prophet and Loss: Salman Rushdie's Migration of Souls," *Voice Literary Supplement,* March 1989, 12; hereafter cited in text as "Prophet."

4. "After the Fatwa," with Clark Blaise, *Mother Jones,* April–May 1990, 31, 65.

5. Roshni Rustomji-Kerns, "Expatriates, Immigrants, and Literature: Three South Asian Women Writers," *Massachusetts Review* 29, no. 4 (September 1988): 657; hereafter cited in text.

6. Emmanuel S. Nelson, "Kamala Markandaya, Bharati Mukherjee, and the Indian Immigrant Experience," *Toronto South Asian Review* 9, no. 2 (Winter 1991): 8.

7. Craig Tapping, "South Asia/North America: New Dwellings and the Past," in *Reworlding,* ed. Nelson, 39, 42. Tapping restricts his paper to the fiction being produced by writers of Indian descent in America, but he could have also mentioned *Mississippi Masala,* Mira Nayar's 1992 film about an Indian American's love for an African American. The themes of Nayar's film—the experience of the diaspora, reworlding, and cross-cultural connections—are also among Mukherjee's major themes.

8. A point that needs to be emphasized here is that Indo-American writing is a fairly recent phenomenon and that Bharati Mukherjee is one of its pioneers. Indeed, in Elaine H. Kim's 1984 bibliographical review of Asian-American writers, Mukherjee is considered to be the only writer of Indian origin working at that time whose fiction dealt with America. See Kim's "Asian American Writers: A Bibliographical Review," *American Studies International* 22, no. 2 (October 1984): 41–78.

9. Shirley Geok-lin Lim, "Twelve Asian American Writers: In Search of Self-Definition," in *Redefining American Literary History,* ed. A. Lavonne Brown Ruoff and Jerry W. Ward, Jr. (New York: Modern Language Association of America, 1990), 246.

10. Shirley Geok-lin Lim, "Assaying the Gold; or, Contesting the Ground of Asian-American Literature," *New Literary History* 24 (1993): 159; hereafter cited in text.

11. "Response: American Fiction," with Robert Boyers, *Salmagundi* 50–51 (Fall 1980–Winter 1981): 155.

12. See, for example, "When White Makes Right" (*Time*, 9 August 1993, 38–40), a feature that brings out the extent to which racism against Asian immigrants has taken root in parts of the United States lately. It should be pointed out in Mukherjee's defense, however, that *The Middleman* story "Loose Ends" and at least one Iowa scene in *Jasmine*, where the heroine and Bud Ripplemeyer visit a bar, record something of the racism experienced by some Asians in America.

Selected Bibliography

PRIMARY WORKS

Novels

The Tiger's Daughter. Boston: Houghton Mifflin, 1971.
Wife. Boston: Houghton Mifflin, 1975.
Jasmine. New York: Viking Penguin, 1989; London: Virago Books, 1989.
The Holder of the World. New York: Alfred A. Knopf, 1993; London: Chatto &
    Windus, 1993.

Short Story Collections

Darkness. Markham, Ontario: Penguin, 1985; London: Virago Books, 1985;
    New York: Penguin Books, 1985.
The Middleman and Other Stories. New York: Viking Penguin, 1988; London:
    Virago Books, 1988.

Nonfiction

Days and Nights in Calcutta. With Clark Blaise. Garden City, N.Y.: Doubleday,
    1977; New York: Penguin Books, 1986.
"Response: American Fiction." With Robert Boyers. *Salmagundi* 50–51 (Fall
    1980–Winter 1981): 153–71.
"A Conversation with V. S. Naipaul." With Robert Boyers. *Salmagundi* 54 (Fall
    1981): 4–22.
"An Invisible Woman." *Saturday Night* 96 (March 1981): 36–40.
Introduction to *Writers of the Indian Diaspora.* Special issue of the *Literary Review*
    29, no. 4 (1986): 400–401.
The Sorrow and the Terror: The Haunting Legacy of the Air India Tragedy. With
    Clark Blaise. Markham, Ontario: Viking Penguin, 1987.
"Immigrant Writing: Give Us Your Maximalists!" *New York Times Book Review,*
    28 August 1988, 1, 28–29.
"Prophet and Loss: Salman Rushdie's Migration of Souls." *Voice Literary
    Supplement,* March 1989, 9–12.
"After the Fatwa." With Clark Blaise. *Mother Jones,* April–May 1990, 61–65.
"A Four-Hundred-Year-Old Woman." *American Studies Newsletter* 29 (January
    1993): 24–26. Also in *The Writer in Her Work*, vol. 2, edited by Janet
    Sternburg, 33–38. New York: W. W. Norton, 1991.

SECONDARY WORKS

Interviews/Profiles

Carb, Alison B. "An Interview with Bharati Mukherjee." *Massachusetts Review* 29, no. 4 (1988): 645–54.
Cincotti, Joseph A. "Same Trip, Opposite Direction." *New York Times Book Review,* 10 October 1993, 7.
Connell, Michael; Jessie Grearson; and Tom Grimes. "An Interview with Bharati Mukherjee." *Iowa Review* 20, no. 3 (Spring 1990): 7–32.
Conquering America with Bharati Mukherjee. Videocassette. Produced by Bill Moyers. Public Affairs Television, 1990.
Hancock, Geoff. "An Interview with Bharati Mukherjee." *Canadian Fiction Magazine* 59 (May 1987): 30–44.
Healey, Beth. "Mosaic vs. Melting Pot." *New York Times Book Review,* June 1988, 22.
Meer, Ameena. "Bharati Mukherjee." *BOMB* 29 (1989): 46–47.
Steinberg, Sybil. "Immigrant Author Looks at U.S. Society." *Publishers Weekly,* 25 August 1989, 46–47.

Book

Nelson, Emmanuel S., ed. *Bharati Mukherjee: Critical Perspectives.* New York: Garland Publishing, 1993. Contains these original essays: Maya Manju Sharma, "The Inner World of Bharati Mukherjee: From Expatriate to Immigrant"; Pramila Venkateswaran, "Bharati Mukherjee as an Autobiographer"; Brinda Bose, "A Question of Identity: Where Gender, Race and America Meet in Bharati Mukherjee"; Samir Dayal, "Creating, Preserving, Destroying: Violence in Bharati Mukherjee's *Wife* and *Jasmine*"; Janet M. Powers, "Sociopolitical Critique as Indices and Narrative Voice and Gender Codes in Bharati Mukherjee's *Jasmine*"; Pushpa N. Parekh, "Telling Her Tale: Narrative Voice and Gender Roles in Bharati Mukherjee's *Jasmine*"; Anindo Roy, "The Aesthetics of an (Un)willing Immigrant: Bharati Mukherjee's *Days and Nights in Calcutta* and *Jasmine*"; Alpana Sharma Knippling, "Towards an Investigation of the Subaltern in Bharati Mukherjee's *The Middleman and Other Stories* and *Jasmine*"; Debjani Banerjee, "'In the Presence of History': The Representation of Past and Present Indias in Bharati Mukherjee's Fiction"; Gurleen Grewal, "Born Again American: The Immigrant Consciousness in *Jasmine*"; Mitali R. Pati, "Love and the Indian Immigrant in Bharati Mukherjee's Short Fiction"; Carol Stone, "The Short Fictions of Bernard Malamud and Bharati Mukherjee." To date, the only published work on Mukherjee and indispensable for any student of her work. Some of the essays are hostile toward Mukherjee, but others are quite enthusiastic. The volume, however, tends to highlight *Jasmine* at the expense of Mukherjee's early novels and short fiction.

Articles and Reviews

Alam, Fakrul. "From the Aloofness of Expatriation to the Exuberance of Immigration: Mukherjee's Progress." In *Migrations, Migrants, and the United States,* edited by Niaz Zaman and Kamal Uddin Ahmed, 122–34. Dhaka: Bangladesh Association for American Studies Publications, 1992. Survey of Mukherjee's treatment of the immigrant theme.

Appiah, K. Anthony. Review of *The Holder of the World. New York Times Book Review,* 10 October 1993, 7.

Boxill, Anthony. "Women and Migration in Some Short Stories of Bharati Mukherjee and Neil Bissoondath." *Literary Half-Yearly* 32, no. 2 (July 1991): 43–50.

Bradbury, Patricia. Review of *Darkness. Quill and Quire* 51, no. 8 (August 1985): 43.

Casey, Ethan. "*The Holder of the World.*" *Magill's Literary Annual,* edited by Frank N. Magill, 401–405. Pasadena, Calif.: Salem Press, 1994. Appreciative reading of the novel.

Chua, C. L. "Passages from India: Migrating to America in the Fiction of V. S. Naipaul and Bharati Mukherjee." In *Reworlding: The Literature of the Indian Diaspora,* edited by Emmanuel S. Nelson, 51–61. Westport, Conn.: Greenwood Press, 1992. Compares the way in which Naipaul and Mukherjee treat "the uneasy passage of Asian Indians" as they attempt to live the American dream.

Crane, Ralph J. "Of Shattered Pots and Sinkholes: Female Identity in Bharati Mukherjee's *Jasmine.*" Paper presented at the sixth SPACLALS Triennial Conference in Freemantle, Western Australia, 9–11 December 1992. Unpublished treatment of *Jasmine* as a female bildungsroman.

Desai, Anita. Review of *Darkness. London Magazine,* December 1985 and January 1986, 143–46.

Erskine, Thomas. "*The Middleman and Other Stories.*" In *Magill's Literary Annual,* edited by Frank N. Magill, 553–57. Pasadena, Calif.: Salem Press, 1989. Discusses the stories of the collection as metaphorical treatments of the conflicts faced by Asian Indians as they settle in North America.

Gorra, Michael. Review of *Jasmine. New York Times Book Review,* 10 September 1989, 9.

Jain, Jasber. "Foreignness of Spirit: The World of Bharati Mukherjee's Novels." *Journal of Indian Writing in English* 13, no. 2 (July 1985): 12–19. An unsympathetic account of the early work by a leading Indian critic.

Kellman, Steven J. "*Jasmine.*" In *Magill's Literary Annual,* edited by Frank N. Magill, 450–53. Pasadena, Calif.: Salem Press, 1990. An enthusiastic overview of the novel.

Kim, Elaine. "Asian American Writers: A Bibliographical Review." *American Studies International* 22, no. 2 (October 1984): 41–77. Bibliographical survey of the field of Asian-American writing, but mentions Mukherjee's work only in a footnote.

Klass, Rosanne. Review of *Wife*. *Ms.*, October 1975, 83.

Leong, Liew-Geok. "Bharati Mukherjee." In *International Literature in English: Essays on the Modern Writers,* edited by Robert L. Ross, 487–500. New York: St. James Press, 1991. Competent overview of Mukherjee's work as stories of displacement and Americanization.

Levin, Martin. Review of *The Tiger's Daughter. New York Times Book Review,* 2 January 1972, 16.

Lim, Shirley Geok-Lin. "Twelve Asian American Writers: In Search of Self-Definition." In *Redefining American Literary History,* edited by A. Lavonne Brown Ruoff and Jerry W. Ward, Jr., 237–50. New York: Modern Language Association of America, 1990. Although the essay does not consider Mukherjee, it discusses the major motifs of Asian-American writing.

_____ . "Assaying the Gold; or, Contesting the Ground of Asian-American Literature." *New Literary History* 24 (1993): 147–69. Indispensable study of the contexts and evolution of Asian-American writing with brief comments on Mukherjee's place in the Asian-American tradition.

Malik, Amin. "Insider/Outsider Views on Belonging: The Short Stories of Bharati Mukherjee and Rohintan Mistry." In *Short Fiction in the New Literatures in English,* edited by J. Bardolph, 189–96. Nice: Faculte des Lettres et Sciences Humaines, 1989. Juxtaposes Mukherjee's short fiction with that of an important Indian-Canadian writer.

Messud, Claire. Review of *The Holder of the World. Times Literary Supplement,* 12 November 1993, 23.

Nazareth, Peter. "Total Vision." *Canadian Literature* 110 (Fall 1986): 184–91. Although basically a review of *Darkness,* Nazareth is able to comment on the stories collected in the volume in some detail.

Nelson, Cecil. "New Englishes, New Discourses, New Speech Acts." *World Englishes: Journal of English as an International Language* 10, no. 3 (Winter 1991): 317–23. Considers Mukherjee's work from a linguistic perspective and as part of a new discourse.

Nelson, Emmanuel S. "Kamala Markandaya, Bharati Mukherjee, and the Indian Immigrant Experience." *Toronto South Asian Review* 9, no. 2 (Winter 1991): 1–9. Incisive comments on *Darkness* but also helpful because of its generalization on the themes of immigrant fiction.

Pandya, Sudha. "Bharati Mukherjee's *Darkness*: Exploring the Hyphenated Identity." *Quill* 2, no. 2 (December 1990): 68–73. Consideration of Mukherjee's position as a writer joining two disparate worlds.

Raban, Jonathan. Review of *The Middleman and Other Stories. New York Times Book Review,* 19 June 1988, 1, 22–23.

Rajan, Gita. "Bharati Mukherjee." In *Writers of the Indian Diaspora: A Bio-Bibliographical Critical Sourcebook,* edited by Emmanuel S. Nelson, 235–42. Westport, Conn.: Greenwood Press, 1993. Brief but thoughtful survey of Mukherjee's works in a volume devoted to writers of the Indian diaspora.

Review of *The Tiger's Daughter, Times Literary Supplement,* 29 June 1973, 736.

Ross, Robert. "*Darkness.*" *Magill's Literary Annual,* edited by Frank N. Magill, 194–97. Pasadena, Calif.: Salem Press, 1986. Includes brief but percipient comments on all the stories of the collection.

Rustomji-Kerns, Roshni. "Expatriates, Immigrants, and Literature: Three South Asian Women Writers." *Massachusetts Review* 29, no. 4 (Summer 1988): 655–65. Somewhat superficial consideration of Mukherjee as well as Santhia Rama Rao and Kamala Markandaya as South Asian women writers "recreating in their writings the lives of immigrants and expatriates."

St. Andrews, B. A. "Co-Wanderers Kogawa and Mukherjee: New Immigrant Writers." *World Literature Today* 66, no. 1 (1992): 56–58. Brief but helpful comments on Mukherjee's recent stance as a new immigrant writer.

Sandler, Linda. Review of *Wife. Saturday Night,* October 1975, 75–76.

Sant-Wade, Arvinda (and Karen Marguerite Ridell). "Refashioning the Self: Immigrant Women in Bharati Mukherjee's New World." *Studies in Short Fiction* 29, no. 1 (Winter 1992): 11–17. Succinct consideration of the major theme of Mukherjee's later fiction.

Shulman, Polly. Review of *The Middleman and Other Stories. Voice Literary Supplement,* June 1988, 19.

Sivaramakrishna, M. "Bharati Mukherjee." In *Indian English Novelists,* edited by Madhussudan Prasad, 71–86. New Delhi: Sterling, 1982. An early and not very helpful estimate of Mukherjee's work by an Indian critic.

Spurling, John. Review of *The Tiger's Daughter. New Statesman,* 6 July 1975, 155–57.

Tapping, Craig. "South Asia/North America: New Dwellings and the Past." In *Reworlding: The Literature of the Indian Diaspora,* edited by Emmanuel S. Nelson, 35–42. Westport, Conn.: Greenwood Press, 1992. Very good estimate of the phenomenon of North American-South Asian writing. Defends Mukherjee's stance on immigration and expatriation from a fresh and interesting angle.

Vaid, Krishna Baldev. Review of *Wife. Fiction International* 4–5 (1975): 155–57.

Ward, Elizabeth. Review of *The Middleman and Other Stories. Washington Post Book World,* 3 July 1988, 3, 9.

Index

The Author

Fakrul Alam is chair of the Department of English at the University of Dhaka and also director of the institution's Centre for Advanced Research in the Humanities. He has an M.A. from Simon Fraser University and did his doctoral studies at the University of British Columbia. The author of *Daniel Defoe: Colonial Propagandist* (1989), he has contributed to such works as *Writers of the Indian Diaspora* (1993) and *R. K. Narayan: Contemporary Critical Essays* (1993). He has also published essays on Defoe, Melville, Kipling, Lawrence, Rushdie, and American literary history in a variety of journals. Among his forthcoming publications are essays on Edward Said in *Edward Said and the World* (1995) and Nirad Chaudhuri in *Ideas of Home: Literature of Asian Immigration/Emigration*. From 1989 to 1991 he was a Fulbright scholar-in-residence and visiting associate professor at Clemson University, South Carolina.

The Editor

Frank Day is a professor of English at Clemson University. He is the author of *Sir William Empson: An Annotated Bibliography* and *Arthur Koestler: A Guide to Research*. He was a Fulbright Lecturer in American literature in Romania (1980–81) and in Bangladesh (1986–87).